Table of Contents

I Dare You to Walk in my Shoes

Volume One: Getting to the Route of All Evil (Hell)

Volume Two: Redeem the Dream 33 (Heaven)

Volume Three: Rev Me Up 33 (Eternity)

By Ms. Lori Eve Tatarsky
aka Sarai London Tailor

To all the travelers that have been passengers and
drivers with me on this windy and long Route 33
Continue to travel on
Keep putting positive energy and fuel into the car
All of us are to travel far.
We'll see extraordinary and unique scenery along
the way
Don't speed and stop to recharge the battery
Live life with passion and large
Our final destination is "Revelation Station" where
all your life's identity will be reviewed and revealed
All your pertinent information
If you feel you are lost on your way use your GPS
(God Protective Services)
Make sure you don't choose to take the Highway to
Hell Route 666
It ends in the woods with firetrucks, ditches in the
road, pitfalls and potholes
It is where we ultimately become lost souls

*

I dedicate this book to all the lost souls in the
universe. May you, too, be willing to go to any
extremes to recapture the innocent playtime and
euphoric freedom of childhood.

Psalm 139 says that before we were born "all the days ordained for us were written in (His) book."

To my brave readers, enjoy the read. More importantly, enjoy the ride!

With much love and prayers,

Ms. Sarai London Tailor

Acknowledgments

To Queen Sophia, King Blake, Prince Garrett, all habitating in the Royal Parliament Castle. I will never forget, nor have the cardio-capillaries in my heart stop dancing to the many rhythms of your music for making our home a blessed and happy one. I will hold all the memories dear in my jewel-crowned treasure trunk. Every day that we are fortunate enough to be given breath, we collarborate while creating vivid dreams. Most importantly, we thrive and revive from the ominous darkness and live in the Godspeed light, we are alive.

To my amazing go-to girls, Lauren and Liv, you are extraordinary and beyond gifted! All my love and gratitude, for a job well done.

Liv Mammone, Editor in Chief:
oliviamammone@gmail.com

Lauren Espero, Web Developer and Illustrator:
ljadespejo@gmail.com

A Note

Some lines, ideas, or pieces may repeat throughout the volumes. These repetitive experiences, concepts, and material, are intended to give the reader a variety of perspectives, viewpoints, observations, and theory.

Some of the pieces that appear here have been published previously, most in earlier versions, on the blog at the author's website at loritatarsky.com.

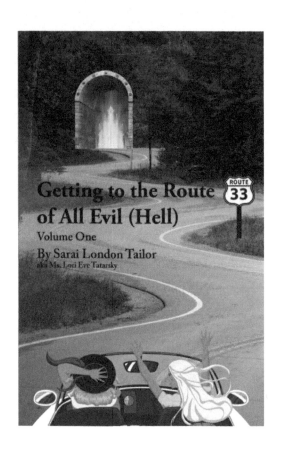

Getting to the Route of
All Evil
(Hell)

It became apparent that the Great I Am had become the parent, not just the Son. While on my journey, I had my navigation GPS (God's Protective Services) The road was long. At times windy with bumps in the road and potholes. I headed to those that were reckless drivers and pointed them in a new direction of resurrection and peace. I stopped at red lights and took in the endless sights. I gloriously would go through the lights of Green. magnificent sights unforeseen. The adventure travels on, there is no end. Eternity is around the corner.

Sarai's Glory Story

Allow me to introduce myself, I am respectfully Ms. Tailor. On my god given mission, it wasn't always a walk in the park. I delightfully liked to greet people and engage in conversations. Was it more convenient to complain, vent and squark?

I loved everyone unconditionally, yet veered away from the negative energy. This is primarily who I would be. Perhaps while sipping my Earl Gray tea and eating my English crumpets; the beautiful classical music around coming from the blessed trumpets.

I went from riches to rags; carelessly and foolishly spending all of my money. Yet I knew in my heart of hearts that eventually once again it would be vividly sunny. Throughout my travels, I lost an unheard of amount of money and weight. All of my young skin would begin to sag. What about all those that fought for our country and are willing to bow down to their country's flag. Throw the garbage and negative issues away. Be grateful for fresh purified air each and every day without horrors or penalty. The more you are accountable for your actions, the more you shall clearly see. Ms. Tailor went back to rags from riches. I blame my loss on those evil doers and those that came into my territory. They were real sons of bitches. The pendulum swings fast and furious. God willing, I would remain wealthy for all the world's eyes to witness and see. I would try to not have resentment against those sons of bitches. What I learned was that it was more cathartic to continue to laugh and wind up in stitches. Being famous is strictly a state of mind, no different than being infamous. It's how you play or play out the game. I chose to step up to the plate and no matter how many foul balls I hit. I would eventually hit a grand slam. When the bases were loaded and my team—the LA Angels—would be the victors.

Good day! I was born Sarai London Tailor and I arrived on this planet January 10[th,] 1972. I was two and a half months premature and my mother was operated on in an emergency C-section. It left a large scar on my mother and she wondered if she would be scarred for life. Even on my best days, I was a handful. I was more than excited to begin my life journey. I would work and adhere to idolatry. God was always the first in line and the chief executive officer. My boss that I worked for was overall fair. Yet sometimes, I questioned His actions. The good thing was he didn't believe in minimum wage. He believed in helping you to become a top producer. I know my gracious host, God, has a unique adventure planned for me, it was just a matter of me getting on board.

My beautiful mother, Sophia, took up horseback riding around the time I was born. I guess She surmised that she needed a relaxing hobby to endure the stress of me being born along with my older brother, Garrett. She turned into a fine equestrian, showing all over. She even took part in the Hampton Classic. She was a vision in her riding gear, a true vision.

It was my pleasure to meet my father. He was handsome, loving, charismatic, and loyal. He was total joy. His name was Blake Elliot Tailor and he would provide me with a childhood that the ancient angels couldn't even imagine.

Early childhood was a ball of never ending fun. Meeting my whole family, each one of them was a character in their own right. They added so much bliss to my awakening days. Something that sticks out in my mind is sharing the holidays with family. I particularly liked Russia Homa, which is really Rosh Hashanah. I would always love to rush home for it. HA! My brother, Garrett, and I would pretend we were Donny and Marie Osmand and put on a show for everyone. Gratuity was gladly accepted. Yet they didn't throw dollar bills or have us sign a contract.

I would travel with Blake to his antique stores in his Cadillac Seville and devilles. We would listen to our favorites, Frank Sinatra, ol' blue eyes, and Barbara Streisand. It made us feel higher than any hallucinogen or alcohol. We would sing along and move our bodies to the rhythm of the enchanting sounds of these two iconic performers. It was at work with Blake that I would become a full-fledged business woman. He would teach me about fine art and having an eye for it. He would show me how to build a rapport and allure for the clients. He would teach me about the importance of negotiation, yet how to always make a profit. After work, we would go to a nearby bar, restaurant called Panama Hatties. I would sit at the bar like a real young lady and repetitively drink Shirley Temples while Blake would engage in his Jack Daniels. It was no less intriguing to go with Blake to the antique stores than to spend time at Sotheby's. Blake would wink at me when he made a sale on a very expensive piece and tell me, "stick with me kid, I will make you a star."

Blake would travel to Paris eight times a year and bring back large containers of antiques, not to mention designer clothes for Sophia and me. It was like being a fashion model in a vogue fashion magazine. During the summer months, the entire family would spend time in the backyard furnild with a large underground pool. Garrett and I would see how high we could dive off of the diving board. We would bask in the sunlight for hours until we turned bright red like tomatoes.

I was growing up quickly; becoming my own woman with my own values, opinions, and morals. God was shaping my identity. I was becoming a unique individual and no one would rain on my parade. In my travels, people would say that I had a personality like Barbara Streisand. This was enough to put me on a brass pedestal.

Junior high was a life changing experience. I would make so many friends that I was voted most popular. What a prestigious honor! I loved taking my friends and introducing them to other friends. It was like being on a ferris wheel or merry go round at Adventure Land. Everyone would spin around like the globe was spinning, not quite sure where it would stop. Yet everyone was together as one. It was truly a blessed experience. There was so much love to be distributed. But I was realizing that even though love was so beautiful, it was so hard to maintain, sustain, and obtain. With strong love also came occasional dislike and hate. One instance that, to this day at age forty eight, still gnaws at my soul and puts a blockage in my heart, was one day Sophia was cleaning the house. I was out of control with my temper tantrums. I wanted what I wanted when I wanted it. There was no reasoning with me. Sophia was forced into taking action. She would pull me by the hair down the hallway and call me a cunt. The only thing I thought was, *I must have deserved it. I am a spoiled runt.*

I questioned what was worse: physical or emotional abuse. I believed they were comparable. But at least the marks from physical abuse would heal. The repercussions from the emotional abuse would linger onward and upward. What I realized from a young age was that no human being had the right to abuse any other human being. If they chose to be abusive, they could self-abuse and beat themselves up. Yet ultimately, everything in life is a choice. So please choose wisely.

In my young life, I would get my period. It was a bloody mess. It would leave me with mood swings that equated to <u>PMS</u> (permissible manslaughter). I wondered why men didn't experience this. But after all, men could be castrated.

During vacations from school, I would spend time in Florida with my relatives. It was total bliss and utopia. We would spend time at the five-star hotels, such as The Fountain Blue. We would go to shows, dine out, lay on the beaches, play in the waves, have meals at each person's home, and just collectively bounce off each other's positive energy. To top off this adventure among ventures, Blake would take Garrett and I to the country club to play golf. As far as Blake went, it was a par for the course. Me and Garrett would get a hole in one. The *piece de resistance* would be when Blake would teach his offspring to play poker. Even when the chips were down, they would continue upward. Blake was precise and would get a royal flush. It had nothing to do with the toilet bowl.

It was supposed to be my sweet sixteen, but the only thing that happened was a paralyzing dream. All I wanted to do was to be in hysterics and scream. Six years prior, Blake had quadruple bypass open heart surgery at the St. Vincent's hospital in Manhattan. In some sort of strange way, he suffered the consequences of being the life of the party. Blake enjoyed his liquor, his cigarettes, his fine foods that weren't always healthy. The day of dichotomy and devastation had arrived. After a six year incubation period, Blake was diagnosed with the deadly AIDS virus. It crippled him, emancipated him, and caused agonizing pain.

It was my senior year of high school, a year that was supposed to be filled with utter exhilaration. Homecoming, Prom, looking at colleges. Yet I was numbed to all this because my superhero, Blake, was losing his special powers. Ironically, on my seventeenth birthday, January 10th, 1989, Blake took his last breath on this plane called mother earth. I was the last person to speak with him.

"Princess, when I get out of here I will buy you whatever you want for your birthday."

All I wanted was not to feel lost and abandoned. I wanted to continue staring into his deep blue eyes and witness his endearing smile from cheek to cheek.

At Blake's funeral, there was a mass of people. I read the eulogy, then reflected on how unfair it was that the kingdom had taken his kind soul at such an early age of forty seven. What I realized was that regardless of how old you are at your passing, what it comes down to is the time you are allotted. How many lives do you build up with compliments and confidence as opposed to tearing them down with insults and negativity. It could be as catastrophic as the tearing down of the twin towers on 9/11. While on this planet, how many lives will you impact in a positive light? How many souls did you surge? How many hearts did you dance with until the small hours of the morning?

Jesus Christ is a perfect example of this. He was brutalized and crucified at age thirty three. From the ages of thirty to thirty three, he preached and performed miracle after miracle. In many ways, although we do not bleed outwardly or have been hung on a cross, we bleed within as humans and are crucified from the heartaches and traumas of our lives. In some semblance, we do experience a resurrection and rebirth.

I and my many friends had graduated high school and were on our way to college. We were like a flock of seagulls flying and dispersing in different directions, yet in synchronicity with each other, eventually meeting in the great paradoxical skies. Many of them dream of the same reality, a thriving career, marriage, children, a home, the ability to live and to follow our passions with enduring purpose. I attended a private college in Boca Raton, Florida. It was referred to as College of Boca Raton or Children Born Rich. I was a double major in mass communications and journalism. I envisioned one day communicating to the masses or becoming like a Katie Couric. I loved the freedom of being on my own. I was evolving, good, bad or different, as a lady of my word. Not to mention I loved the power of words. I enjoyed puns, plays on words, essays, stories, riddles, rhymes etc. I studied hard to have a vast vocabulary and to be well poised and articulate. One of my favorite things at college was to spend time in the library. I was enamored by all the books. I veered towards the non-fiction stories. I absolutely, no questions asked, loved learning about other people's life journeys. In many respects, I could relate. Essentially, we are all students and teachers at different venues of our path. Forever learning, forever evolving, forever changing.

It was spring break at school and one of my good friends was having a party in Pikesville, Maryland. I ingested a tab of acid and I would go on a trip that was far from first class. I recklessly drove home to Long Island doing a hundred and twenty miles per hour in her sports car. When I, by the grace of God, got home, it was there that I would meet my opponent, my deceiver, my arch rival and enemy. Could it be Satan? I was heavily delusional and thought Satan was possessing me. I fell into a deep, devastating depression. It was then that I was told I had bipolar type one with psychotic features.

I was damaged, plagued with a chronic mental illness. My whole world crumbled. When you have a taste of the good life, you develop severe heartburn and indigestion when it all fades away. I was unable to finish college. One of my biggest fears was abandonment. Yet, wasn't it I, Sarai, that abandoned all of my high school and college friends? I didn't even give them a chance to still love and accept me. The negative stigma of

20

mental illness was a fortress of failure. I was afraid. I would now be viewed and judged as stupid, uneducated, and ignorant.

In my early twenties, I made a decision to uproot my life and move to Houston, Texas. I had discovered a treatment center for mentally ill people that was focused on recovery and their well-being. There, I would study under an innovative spiritual mentor. Below is the letter I had written to her mother.

Mummie Dearest,
It was quite the tiresome trip to Texas but something I felt I had to do. My life back home left me nothing but despair, shame, and emptiness when I left more than four years ago. Although I have a severe condition if not properly addressed with medication and therapy, I thank God that I am not as sick or helpless as these people in the group home. So much of the time I want to help and understand them so I find it comforting to be in their company. I want to cry out for their healing. Most of them are so lonely and sad, have very few friends, and spend most of their days doped up on high doses of medication, smoking cigarettes, and sleeping. For some, it's a stepping stone, yet primarily for most it's their unintended long-term home. Most of them can't take care of themselves on their own. They are like lost children in a field of wilted weeds and darkness.

I, too, at times have felt this helplessness, hopelessness, and unhappiness. I, too, at times have felt so alone, so scared, unheard, incapable, and unworthy. Yet, by the grace of God, I have risen time and time again. I will never stop giving back to these people who can never give to themselves. However, that doesn't contradict how out of place I feel here. I still possess resentment and anger knowing that my own mother, who I have loved and will always love through everything, could actually allow me to be in a homeless shelter or more-or-less outpatient hospital for the mentally ill. I never meant to cause you pain nor distress or to be a burden. Yet I never asked for this infliction of mental illness. I myself have been dying from within for so very long and just wish that you and I could have a special relationship with no major conditions. By the mere fact that you gave me life and so much love, I will always be indebted to you, yet it's a crying shame that you never could understand the Belle Essence of who I truly am!

I love you now and forever,
Your Baby Girl
"Lori Belle"

My time spent in Texas was more or less a disaster. It was filled with many gut wrenching states of mania. I was promiscuous with any strange men I would allow in my apartment. I was so reckless while driving that it led to a major accident, leaving me in a brace from a broken back. I had so many spending sprees that I was left in financial ruin and had to file bankruptcy for a hundred thousand dollars. At one point, I was on a business trip to Dallas at a five-star hotel. It was there that I was handcuffed and arrested for criminal trespassing. I had made so many severe mistakes while merely existing in Texas that I wild I could rectify.

I yearned for once upon a time when I was happy and at peace with myself. For the most part, I was living a very lonely reclusive life with the exception of interaction with my therapist and my therapist's family.It was after that pondering and strong remembrance that I knew in the depths of my soul that it was time for me to head back to New York and begin anew. It was 1999, almost an entire new decade.

I settled in the beautiful Westchester, New York; not too far from my mother and my mother's boyfriend, Joshua. I had seen a help wanted ad for an advertising account executive with the Gannett Journal News. I had no experience, nor a college degree. But I did have an illuminating personality that equated to a masters degree or doctorate in Who Could Bullshit the Bullshit Artist. I had become a ham and that suited me well. My loved ones referred to me as Lori Belle. Whoever didn't like it could pork off or kiss my tuchas (ass) in Macy's window. I met with the CEO and charmed the pants off of him. In reality, I had no desire to see his jockey briefs. I showed so much inquisitiveness and excitement for this new opportunity that I would be hired.

This started my fifteen year long complex yet riveting career in advertising. I loved going to work every day. It was more like playtime with no curfew. I loved to dress to impress; wearing vintage hats, scarves, designer suits, silk shirts. It was like going to the Oscars. My colleagues and bosses were also dressed to the nines. One had to look good to go into the barracks, into combat and had to consistently drum up business. Together as a strong resourceful team, we made up a constellation of stars. Some shined bright. Some were dimmer, yet they all added to the twilight. Then morning would arrive with clouds but a rainbow appeared. Then, majestically, the sultry sun would turn the sky so blue that it bordered on periwinkle and off I went to the office for a new daily adventure. I loved meeting and dining with clients, discussing how to creatively bring in more revenue which would ultimately enrich their lives. We would dine at fancy restaurants and have drinks such as cosmopolitans, fine wines, virgin bloody Mary's. (Just a quick thought: was the virgin Mary really a virgin? Only Joseph could divulge the truth and he was site unseen.) I worked hard and made a lot of money. I devised ways of writing things off on my taxes, such as dining with clients and vacations. I even maneuvered a way to write off my dry cleaning and laundry. I never liked her uncle Sam. He took so much of my earnings, it was almost like an embezzlement. After all he was a distant relative! Why couldn't he stay far away? A series of times, I was a top producer. Yet by the same token, there were plenty of times that I was in the slumps.

I came to realize that the advertising area wasn't in my best interest or conducive for my bipolar disorder. There were too many ups and downs; highs and lows. The pressure to produce and meet quotas and deadlines became unbearable. The career I chose caused me many periods of depression, mania, and hospitalization in mental institutions. For the most part, I was only able to stay at each job for two to three years before I would lose my job and experience pandemonium. Then that dark day would materialize and my life would be changed forever.

I had negative thoughts ruminating in my mind.

I am not good enough. I am a burden on my friends and family. I can't hold down a job. No man will truly ever love and accept me because of my mental illness. I will never experience the

*exhilaration and happiness of having children and
being a mother or grandmother.*

I ingested bottles of my psychiatric pills and
was rushed to the nearest hospital. This was my first
suicide attempt. Yet surely not the last. I developed
a common condition called compartment syndrome
which the doctors kept misdiagnosing. They waited
eleven hours to do surgery. They must have been on
an extended lunch break at my expense. I was left
with what you call a drop foot or a permanent limp.
Through all that, I was ever so grateful that they
didn't have to amputate my leg or that I wasn't
confined to a wheelchair. Yet how would I ever
survive the harshness and judgment of the world?
Not only did I have a mental disability , now I had a
physical disability. Maybe this was God's way of
telling me to slow down. Up until this point, I was a
mover and a shaker to such a degree that I
constantly had anxiety attacks. God didn't want me
to miss the astounding, colorful gardens that were
waiting for me.

I sued the hospital for malpractice. I found
myself a top-notch Manhattan lawyer who knew all
the ins and outs of justice. He would go against the
joker and pull out the wild card. One nation under
God indivisible and justice for all. I walked away
with 400,000 dollars. 100,000 I would give to my
mother, Sophia. That was barely enough to cover all
of the financial conundrums I had gotten myself
into. I gave 10,000 dollars to my brother and sister
in law so they could enjoy themselves after working

so hard. I was left with 290,000 dollars that I pissed away within a three year period. I still hadn't learned that money doesn't grow on trees. Eventually, the hurricane would occur. Not only would the branches come down, so would the trees.

Overall, I had a full and contented life in Westchester. While living there, I had many real and wonderful friends and business contacts. I explored many of my passions such as acting, writing, advocating, entrepreneurship, and comedy improv classes. I was drawn to the melodrama of acting. I thought with the comedy improv, I may not become a stand-up comedian. But it was still on the table that I could become a sit-down comedian. I explored my religious beliefs and became a messianic Jew, which many people believed was a mess of a Jew. Basically, I would follow my Jewish roots but believed Jesus was the Messiah. One of my greatest accomplishments came when I would volunteer for MHA (Mental Health Association). I would give lectures about my experiences with mental illness. I only wanted to heal the wounded and give them strength and hope. I was certainly not the pope yet I loved being on the pulpit. At times, my voice could be loud and boisterous. But it was out of enthusiasm to be heard and acknowledged. We lived in such times that people wouldn't really pay attention to one another. Their people skills were squandered. It was all about social media. People would constantly be on Facebook, Instagram, or Twitter. People would be emailing constantly or texting or watching YouTube. I prayed my thoughts were synchronized with my audience and my words were making a positive difference.

One of the things I was happiest about was that my mother had found someone to wholeheartedly love again. Joshua was from the old school. He was handsome, kind, and funny. No one would ever replace my father but Joshua was a close second. Joshua, from the depths of his being, loved and worshiped the ground Sophia walked on. He supplied a lavish lifestyle: fine dining, traveling the world, eighteen karat jewelry, clothes, and cars. *La crème de la crème* was when Joshua bought Sophia a $30,000 horse from Germany. She would ride every day with joy in her heart and soul.

The year was 2015. I was utterly broke and went through my lawsuit money with nothing to show but a good time. I had lost my current job and my mental illness returned like a wrecking ball. I was on the verge of eviction and could no longer afford the high end gated community I lived in. I was in such a deep depression that I would lay in bed to the point of urinating; smoking until there were large holes in the mattress. Sophia was so supportive and gracious that she invited me to come live with her in her one bedroom apartment. There was no way I was going back to a group home. It was true that I adored group therapy. Yet ultimately, I was defiant and never wanted to live in a group home again. So I went off with my mother. Now I was under her roof obeying her rules as if I was a child again. It was more than difficult living as a forty four year old woman under the constraints of my senior aged mother. I was used to my independence. I had lived on my own for much of my adult life. My mother now resided in a co-op with full amenities in Bayside, Queens. She had been there for several years. She had even lost her soulmate, Joshua, many years prior to kidney failure. I always wanted to console her for losing the two loves of her life. Sophia always answered that she felt cheated and wondered how fantabulous her days on earth would have been if my father and Joshua hadn't passed away.

I missed my loved ones and relatives so very much. I missed their touch. I constantly pondered what occurred once they arrived at the pearly gates. It must have been their time to go. It might have been fate. I dreamed of heaven. I imagined everyone who passed would reside in their own mini-mansions yet be connected to their neighbor's house. All of these heavenly souls and spirits would frolic and play. Each one of them would have their own big screen TV and, with the remote, they could see all of their loved ones who were left on planet Earth. They could see their every action and guide them through the difficult traumatic times into bliss.

When I moved to Bayside I was put on AOT. This basically meant I was mandated to take medication and attend a day treatment program. That was the best decision that Judge Judy could have made. The name of the treatment center was Goodlife Baruch Haim (Thank God). The staff was amazing. All they wanted to do was to heal the sick, wounded, and damaged. They would look you in the eyes with such love and comfort. It really was true that the eyes are the window to the soul. The only contradiction to this statement was that some of the clients were so sick that their windows were deadbolted. I befriended many of the clients and I felt well understood, accepted, and safe. I felt like they were family. We were each battling our own mental illness. No one was better or worse. We were just in it together. Together we stand, divided we fall. Then that special day would arrive when I would encounter my new therapist, Jewel.

Jewel's inner being was as sweet as the scent of Chanel Number 5. Her soul radiated like a fine piece of Cartier. To add to her attributes, Jewel was well dressed and well spoken. Jewel would graciously become my Jewel of the Nile. Jewel and I had a strong rapport and understood one another. But the boundaries that Jewel set were extremely difficult for me to abide by. In the past, my first therapist in Texas was like a surrogate mother to me. With my next therapist, I would take her kids out to IHOP for pancakes. Jewel actually did me a big favor by enforcing the boundaries between therapist and client. It made me more apt to have stronger, deeper relationships with my loved ones by placing boundaries with them and highly respecting their limits. Jewel could always make me smile even in my darkest struggles and strife. I would joke around with Jewel using her off-beat humor. She didn't seem to be amused most of the time and told me I needed new material. Maybe my humor, at times, was more off the wall. I could definitely relate to being off the wall from time to time. Jewel made me work hard at recovery and growth. She made me accountable for my life choices and addressed my habit of forming bad patterns. Jewel would make suggestions to me and guide her. Yet she blatantly told me she couldn't be my Jiminy Cricket. In other words, Jewel couldn't be my conscience. It was just as well because I preferred Minnie and Mickey Mouse.

While I was working with her, Jewel got married to her college sweetheart. I prayed it would be til death do them part. In today's world, the divorce rate skyrockets and the poor children suffer aimlessly and are left scorned. Or some couples would be married ten or twenty years and then tell their partner that they are gay. If it was up to me, I would rather come out of the closet than be held in that prison. Now that Jewel was married, I had premonition that it wouldn't be long before she got pregnant and would be out on maternity leave. I panicked. How could Jewel leave me? Jewel told me that she couldn't be held hostage. No matter how much I worked and prayed to alleviate my fear of abandonment, it would always slap me in the face; leaving metaphoric black and blues. I worried about all my loved ones, especially my mother. If my mother didn't get up at or before seven thirty in the morning , I would check on her to see that I was still breathing. Sophia told me that she wouldn't live forever and to stop acting like a child. Sophia said, in reality I could one day get into a car accident and die.

The blessed day arrived. Jewel told me that she was pregnant and was having a little girl. So this new angel on Earth would be given her mother's fluttering wings and would one day grow into a beautiful loving and strong woman like Jewel. I was so ecstatic about the pregnancy that you could hear my screams of jubilation down the hallway of my apartment. The one thing that saddened me was that, because of strict boundaries set by Jewel, I couldn't be a part of the child's life. Jewel promised to send lots of pictures. I joked that I could be the baby's nanny and would work for minimum wage. In all reality, parents today have to work long hours. Some even take two jobs to comfortably support their families and make ends meet. In many instances, a nanny or relative has to raise the child.

While living with Sophia, I had the creative juices flowing. This was my idea of heaven where I could create literary works and my godly written works with others for their benefit. The book project was so exciting. It brought me YouTube videos where I would talk about the purpose and passion behind the literary project. I met editors, illustrators, transcribers and many others. Once the book was complete, I would self-publish so I wouldn't have to share the proceeds with a publishing house. I put the book on Amazon and sold some copies but at the time the book needed some revisions so I took it down. Then life happened. I wasn't well enough to take on promoting or selling the book. I put the book aside and carried on with heartache. Perhaps it wasn't God's time for me. No matter how much I dreamed about the success of the book, if it was not God's time it wouldn't happen at that moment. I think that stands true for all people's journeys. Some will try to manipulate the system by living on daylight savings time an hour early yet the Creator holds the final stopwatch.

From the time I put the book away, I felt stripped of my creativity. I became envious and somewhat jealous during this timeframe. I had a friend at the treatment center named William. He would write tantalizing poems every day. Each one was more beautiful than the last.

To Lori

*I dream deep, in my daydreams, some of my
fondness for you, my friend. Thank you for so many
hellos and goodbyes in a kind tone of voice. In you,
I see Eden set aloft within the core of my soul.
Daylight always shines within my memories of you,
gentle soul that guides me along.
—William Charles E.*

Obstacles

*Sometimes we are in our own dream's way. We
must clear our paths of ourselves to rise above the
storm. We are what this life holds, be it good or ill.
We make the choice. Let us, instead of lingering in
being stagnant, pursue all of our hopes. Becoming
what life truly holds its best intentions for us
—William Charles E.*

I have gratitude for

*Angelic days that seem, in their loveliness, to go on
forever. Birdsong that reaches my ears in sublime
symphonies. Children's laughter, butterflies on soft
wing that show off their colors to a waiting world,
nature, fireworks, flowers that fill the air with
fragrance as well as color. In short, everything in
the world.
—William Charles E.*

Thank you

*For kindness given within my times in your
company. For the divine light of your presence each
time I rove within daylight. Being a humble man, I
don't ask for help often. You give it to me without as
much as a word from me. In short, thank you for
being a friend.*
-William Charles E.

While residing with my mother, I felt a little
sad. Sophia's life had become simple and slow. The
crux was going to the horse stable. This would keep
her mentally stable. I constantly was horsing
around. I thought it was so endearing that Sophia
would speak to her three close friends every night.
It was better than the Housewives of Beverly Hills;
it was the horse wives of horse manure. They would
spend hours talking about their horses. In some
semblance, I felt comfortable and safe living under
Sophia's roof. I would always say good morning
and good night. It was the first breath I took of the
day and the last.

About a year into living with Sophia, a
wonderful unexpected surprise happened. Someone
on Facebook had mutual friends and contacted him.
His name was Mark and he certainly left a mark on
my life as well as footprints on my heart. He was a
graduate of my high school but graduated a few
years earlier. Our first date was something else. We

spoke fluently for hours. I revealed that I had a mental illness called bipolar and he shared that he suffered from depression. I explained to him that most of my adult relationships were sexcapades and rolls in the hay. I spoke highly of my dad and how much, after almost thirty years, I would still cry; missing him insurmountably. I explained that I never allowed myself to wholeheartedly love another man because I feared loss and abandonment. Mark spoke about his previous marriage and divorce. He also shared that he was bullied from a young age until tenth grade and had a very difficult relationship with his father. As a result of this trauma, he had the need to make sure everybody liked him. It became an obsession to the point where he had 1,000 Facebook friends. I wondered if we ended up together, would he leave me not for another woman but for Facebook?

I could read people like a great American novel. Most of the time, I could see the positive in people. But occasionally to my dismay, I would end up in toxic relationships. The more time I spent with Mark, the more I could see his incredible attributes. He was sensitive to a tee, sweet, loving, funny, interesting, and deep down a kind soul. As things progressed, I could open my chained self to the possibility of true and lasting love. As time went on, I met his family. They were hardworking, accomplished, and very warm hearted. The thing I respected most was the fact that they not only took the time to get to know me, but they took the time to understand and accept my mental illness. I had a special fondness for Mark's mother. She had been a teacher for many years and positively impacted children's lives. I looked to Mark's mom as a mentor of sorts.She and I would have long, deep conversations. I admired and respected her ability to not only be her own woman but also how she was so authentic and cared deeply for her loved ones. I joked with Mark that if I didn't marry him, I would see if I could marry his mom. Throughout the years, I would spend all of the Jewish holidays with Mark's family. It was so much fun but produced a lot of anxiety in me. It was so nostalgic. I would recall spending once upon a time holidays with my own family. During my evolution with Mark and the time spent living with my mother, I was hospitalized for depression and psychosis several times.

That fatal day in October of 2019 snuck up on me. I had just finished ECT (electro convulsive shock treatment) but I wasn't willing to be honest and forthright with my doctors. Days prior, I was having suicidal ideations and the negative banter and commentary in my mind would linger.

I will never work again. My literary words will never be read or spoken. The world would be better off if I was dead. I will never be free from this crippling disease. I am a failure. I am a burden on my family and friends, especially my mother. Mental illness has stripped from me the future of being a mother and raising children.

These falsities were so strong and ruminating that I had no clarity to do a reality check. Meeting of the mind, the mindful, and the mindless.

The conference room of the third floor psych unit opened and I knew it would shake. Sophia entered before the chief of psychiatry, the clinical manager, and the social worker. Mom sat looking more exhausted and more serious than ever. She kept reiterating in a stern, harsh voice that she was so tired and had been through enough pain and heartache over the past thirty years. Now it was about her living out the rest of her life without all this worry and responsibility. After witnessing me near death in her apartment, this last suicide attempt prompted twelve cops to come. I lay still on the floor unresponsive, unconscious and barely breathing. They intubated me to help me breathe and rushed off to the emergency room at the nearest hospital. I was in the ICU for five days in a coma. One cop stayed with my mother in case I didn't make it. When I gratefully opened my eyes, I promised to appreciate the simple things such as a hazelnut iced coffee from Dunkin' Donuts. Holding Mark's, his mother's, and my mother's hands. Looking them all in their eyes and feeling blessed to be alive and part of the planet again. I vowed that even if I took baby steps, I would somehow in some way live a full and happy life.

I felt enormous guilt and shame for my suicide attempt especially to my mother. I wrote her an apology letter such as this title I love you now and forever mother.

I wanted to always be your shining star with dazzle and sparkle. I was raised with so much love and contentment. I felt on top of the world wearing my very own silk slippers. You have been such an incredible mother. No different than a celebrity accepting her academy award year after year. How I failed you over the years with the remnants of mental illness. It stripped me of so many dreams that I wanted to share with you, my bella. Like the first time you were reading me a classic childhood story, I knew I was blessed to have the childhood and family that I did. I felt safe wrapped in my cocoon emerging from a tired and worn out caterpillar to an astounding butterfly. I never meant to cause you pain, worry, or fear. Have I become nothing but a burden on you? I felt like a mouse strapped fiercely to its cage. I never had the essence of being a mother. The joy, the teachings, the love, the lessons, the pain; all of it entangled in a spider's web. I beg you to forgive me for my suicide attempts. I never wanted to hurt myself or you. The loathing banter in my mind raced. I could only imagine in my darkest moments how you felt when you found me overdosed and close to death. I ask that you reach for the stars. Bask in God's sunlight. I know you are the epitome of a good soul. I will always love and appreciate the person you are. When I think of you, my heart beats overtime like a baby's first words.

Each time I had a relapse or a suicide attempt, it would take what seemed like ages to get my grounding back. I would literally have to take it one day at a time. Even one moment at a time, in certain instances. I would have to crawl before I could tap dance again.

About six months after my suicide attempt, my mother sat me down and said we needed to have a serious discussion. Sophia told me that the landlord wanted to give his son the apartment and wasn't renewing the lease. She made a hard decision to move upstate to Kingston in order to have a slower pace and to be near her son and his wife. She asked me if I wanted to join her in Kingston but I denied the offer. I had a full life where I was living. Not to mention I had top notch doctors and therapists here. The more I thought about it, the more I realized my mother and I needed our own private space. We were constantly fighting and arguing face to face. Our whole relationship had become a disgrace. I would miss her mom terribly and didn't know how I would be without her. But I felt that this was a step in the right direction. Sophia was always my biggest supporter and cheerleader and if she left, it could massively impede me. It was time for new chapters in our lives to be read and written by God's right hand.

There were castles and kings and queens; there were magnificent horses to be ridden. The sun was shining so bright, it was gleaming. The stars were twinkling like large karat diamonds. The moon was a freely flowing half crescent. I had been beaten down like a large, swaying, wild tree where the branches are fragmented and weak. My heart was bleeding rapidly from the pain and stigma of mental illness. My soul was suffocating and without breath. The knives were being thrown at me like a shooting gallery, aimlessly and fierce. I had been resurrected in the glorious glow of warmth. Love was spread around like a wild carpet ride with magic and glory. A ray of light was reflecting on the connection of all the people. The heart was beating as quickly as the drums were being creatively and passionately played. Dreams lived on in God's gratitude of gifts.

Redeem the Redeemables

And Jesus said to them, "go into all the world and proclaim the good news to all of creation" (Mark 16:15).

Take two. Now do you know what to do. Don't abuse or threaten me—boo hoo. Redeem the world's dream. There is so much anarchy in this world, it induces rage. Lock Lucifer in his flame induced cage. All enraged. We must turn the page. Don't scream. All of us humans are a team, like an athlete on the beam. Put the guns down. This is no living joke. So many are perishing without hope. Yet some husbands and wives have virtually and remotely eloped. We have much strife in each and every life but the Messiah is here. Be joyful; do not fear even if you are not sincere, my dear. It is our job—no need to cry or sob. Is your full name written in the book of life? And does its log include the animals like the turtles and the frogs? Laugh out loud like a clown. I am wound up, worrying with all of the world's problems and can't sleep. Should I weep? The world is in deep.

You son of a bitch, bury yourself in a dark ditch. Your days are numbered. It's the thirty-third day. I know where you have come from, you nauseating scum. Jesus, Joseph and Mary are now one. There is no room for you in our new place so we will get rid of your presence and erase. We are not scared to see you face to face and look you square in the eyes. We despise your anti biblical lies. What is left for every birth that must live and die? Countless wonders still searching why.

Seven heavenly angels traveled from up above. Their main mission was to prophesize unconditional love. It came from the almighty God all over and above. Flying all over were the sparrows and white light. We can delight. There is more insight banishing fright. If the Messiah came back—what an amazing sight. It would be earthly delight. He was strong even with a small wafer bite. The almighty is never dead or we would dread one day at a time. Venture out of your normal complacent self-sitting in bed.

The pandemic was more like a pan where everyone was boiling and burning. To call this travesty to end is a deep, deep yearning. To continue to go back and to see all the colorful flowers bloom and their soil. Graduations, life celebrations, weddings are all being done virtually. Children once in the classroom now are condemned to zoom. People laid off in droves and business closing because they can't pay the rent. Going belly up. Completely broke. This is no laughing matter. This is no joke. In today's reality, there is social distancing under any circumstances—no affection. No kisses, no hugs, no handshakes. We all must unite together and a forceful team make. It will take this to end this fatality. This is today's reality. Wearing the masks, you can't breathe or see. How could this unfortunate circumstance be? Regardless, if you, he, or I must work feverishly to unlock the gates of Heaven with the key. We need all of the angels circling around the circumference of the globe. Perhaps in our biggest fantasy, Jesus will descend and come down in a fine silk robe. Wouldn't this utterly be alluring to see. We are barely existing in the times of the end. We must work together, do our part, and open our hearts to a new way. A new day.

Hopefully, we will ascend to glory. There will be a new consciousness amongst us of love for ourselves and others; respect for all mankind. For everlasting peace of mind. For every end, there is a new beginning. For all of those people that are evil, greedy, and sinning, you can join your maker—the Grim Reaper—in the pit of fury in Hell. This would ultimately be swell. The fallen angel St. Lucifer fell. The universe would again be left with all the generous, kind, thoughtful playmates galore. All of the diversified birds in the world would be chirping, singing, and soaring. This would inevitably be so alluring. Pouring the anointed water over each individual's head.

Thank you, Almighty, the pandemic is finished. There are no more souls that will instead lose their lives and be dead. We will live infinitely and the world will become one. It will be fun. There will be an overabundance of sun. The people of God would have won.

There will no longer be a reason to escape or run. We will all experience evolution and the new creation. We will be at heights of elation. We will each have a mission to carry out for the kingdom and the almighty there is one God in Heaven that we will come to intrinsically trust. Please clear your eardrums; listen and learn. This is a must. Here He is to bring complete happiness to all the good souls on the earth. In some sense, we will each have a rebirth. Each one of us will recapture our inner child. It will be more enchanting than anything just mild. Your journey through life will be through the curious eyes of a child and you will discover a never-ending source of utopia and euphoria. Curiosity keeps your heart beating; keeps you interested and interesting. It's a whole new world. So join in when the angels sing.

After a long hard day working remotely from home, pick up the cell phone. Call your loved ones to chit chat. Bad reception, the call was dropped. Deceptions from politicians on the clock. Become your own prophet—that's absurd. Would you even know what to speak? What words? So, who will negotiate the deal to end the pandemic? It's a huge ordeal. Escape the harsh reality and fear, drink lots of alcohol and have a Corona beer! When you adapt to this new horrific world, be sincere. We all have fears. The soldiers in the military will put their rifles down. Trump and all the nation's leaders will certainly be given a crown. The virus caused so many to lose their lives and livelihoods. They have brought so many to cry and drown. We fear the ending, resending coronavirus was near. It has left us spiritually drunk, unsure, OD-ing on corona beer. This time, with everyone's input, it will get better. We all must be resilient, help each other, and not bail. Was all of life's journey a fairytale like Dorothy in the Wizard of Oz story? I would be led to glory. Good riddance to all in phase two. You may shop at the mall. It may be an overhaul and recall. The connection lines are open for business for one and for all.

There are winners and losers, yet it's how you play the game which ultimately leads you to the shining star of fame. The winner will have more fun; the losers know who they are. Two drinks minimum. Cash only bar. Drink the anointed water for the son and daughter. We had to take that inmate Satan to the slaughter.

It's thirty three minutes past my bedtime. I love to rhyme! From now on, our planet will have nothing but sunshine. It's a sign of the times. If my book deal doesn't go through, what am I to do? I could always become a blue-collar worker and follow in the footsteps of the Messiah. I could use His carpentry ladder to climb higher and higher, closer to God and the white pearly gates. If it's God's time for me to succeed then it's fate. Nighty night! Don't let the bedbugs bite. Sweet dreams, my little child. Rest easy and don't go wild.

When will the world wake up from the nightmare? This whole pandemic isn't fair.

Countless people dying one day at a time. This certainly is a punishable crime. So much uncertainty each and every day. When will all of the people have enough compassion to heed the guidelines and obey. Citizens exhibiting courage living on the frontlines. This is today's reality and those that do not practice social distancing are subject to social fines. Wearing masks and gloves to protect ourselves and others shows human love. This virus continues spreading. There is so much we have to be dreading. People at the supermarket are forever hoarding. Homeless people falling prey with no boarding. I miss human contact and affection. What does the future hold? Will we overcome with a new, helpful direction of people on lockdown and self-quarantine? Now is the time we must all come together as a resilient team. The economy is sinking at an all-time low. Are we destined to reap what we sow? Covid nineteen, it's nothing like we have seen. A surreal paralyzing crisis. An abomination that feels like a heart attack. We must come together and pray for God's sake. Coronavirus' new normal seems so bizarre. Yet this too shall pass and, as a universe, we will survive and come so far.

Is it safe to smile for a short or long while? We have made it to the miracle mile. Just wear your masks to hide a frown. It's time to give one leader the jeweled crown. Will we re-elect Trump? We must get over the ledge and jump. The election is simultaneous with the Messiah's resurrection. Vote to stay strong. It's a hard decision. Could cause an insurrection. Why is all this despair happening?

Don't know why. Breathe deeply and the Messiah
will, with you, take a long sigh. You don't need
drugs to get high. Perfection is yours to cultivate,
don't fear. Lay back. Without a long ranger mask or
protection. Staying safe will be hard like an erection
some might Climax and cum! Others in danger will
run. Sit away from one another. Ultimately there is
no affection. Hey, what's up brother. Now's the
time to review the New Testament. Start with
revelation. You will instinctively feel a positive
elation.

*

    She was a young, talented dancer. Diagnosis
of stage four cancer. Not even chemo or radiation
would keep her alive. When would the great healer,
God, arrive? Perhaps he was upstairs on a long-
winded break. Keep her alive for God's sake. So
many beautiful children afflicted with some fatal
disease. We must find a way to seize those
travesties. It's not fair, it is more than parents can
bear. The afflicted losing their hair. When will all of
life's diseases come to an end? I pray these God-
awful diseases don't afflict one of my family
members or friends. The loss of life is unbearable
and wrong. Will the loved ones and mourners have
the capacity to stay strong? Will there ever be a
happy ending to all of this pain? Or, ultimately, will
we have to view the death certificate's claim. Claim
the short memories of a short life. We need the staff
and rod for all of this strife. I pray with each new
day that all the world's deadly diseases will decay

away from all these tragedies. I am left heartbroken and speechless. We must all work over time to rectify this mess.

There are so many man-made diseases. We need the miracles performed by Jesus. Here are some to name a few just to give you some insight so you will have a clue. All types of tragic cancers, so many lives stripped away. What is the resolution, the answer? Having a stroke is no longer just for the old folks. With all the stresses we each endure, we are all susceptible to a stroke at our core. Rampant is heart disease God in heaven, we ask, when will it cease. Sufferers worried their hearts will give in. Especially if they are obese and not thin. Back in the 80's, AIDS took so many lives. It was a fight for survival. Mainly gay people died; this just isn't right. My dad was subjected to positive blood during a blood transfusion and contracted AIDS. It was a worldly raid. It took my beloved furiously and fast yet I will always remember this superhero of a dad. And the incredible lessons and memories we shared will eternally last.

Cerebral palsy, Parkinson's, and multiple sclerosis affect all the muscles and bones. Why can't these disabilities leave folks alone? Especially my dear editor and friend, Liv. Its effects are an excruciating reality. Why can't the world wake up and see? It is time we find cures for many illnesses so more humans can live to the fullness of life. Children and loved ones watch their elderly parents suffer with Alzheimer's and dementia. Perhaps it's been so much to bear day to day, year to year. So the mind forgets and blocks out the fear. It's so debilitating to see our loved ones not able to remember. Sometimes, it progresses throughout January to December, the calendar year. Those afflicted with this disease lose, in some cases, their full memory. How on God's good earth can this be? Perhaps it is a theory that their minds have so much pain to remember. I am willing to put a wager on it and bet. So many earthly or man made diseases and disorders that each individual is born with gives them pain. The researchers and doctors have no cures. Now I have been called crazy, but this reality is insane. How many more have to suffer and pass away? We must make health a priority, not tomorrow but today.

Sonya and Joe, my friends, why couldn't your constant kidney dialysis end? On an organ donor list for years, living your life with fear. This painful disease felt like it would last forever. Saving your life was a right endeavor. Unfortunately, you met your demise. Left everybody sad and mourning. Your life ended so quickly without warning.

Diabetes affects blood sugar level. I often wonder if its suffering is sent from the devil. Some people are insulin dependent every day. It has become their life's way. If not treated properly, they can go into a coma or go blind in their eyes. Ultimately, the worst case is they will die.

Mental illness is expansive around the globe and nation. I assure you it's not such a sensation. I have had many episodes of mania and depression. My whole life, my whole being, was in a recession. I came to realize, to a degree, it was about demonic possession. With each new episode, my soul withered away. I was praying for a sun filled day. The disease was clouding up myself and true desires. I vowed I would overcome and set this world on fire.

*

With the grace of God, this will be my last hospitalization. Last days of being in the pen with sickly women and men. Why do I have to suffer so much? I need healing. I need the magic touch. Something to protect me from the night terrors. Why can't it be so simple? And they are construed as pain in the ass errors. Injections given daily to the other inmates. Screaming, bantering, crying, another ordeal. I'm so drugged up, I can't think. I can't feel. I have no words. Now, if you knew me, you would think this is utterly absurd. I have been kidnapped by the beast. I will miss my chair at the holy feast.

I feel like they are going to take me to the electric chair. I didn't even have my six-figure lawyer or a fair trial. My sentence is life in the demon cell. I have been condemned to hell. I am on sick leave on an unpaid vacation. I still feel dead with no emotion or bodily sensation. Look at the bright side, my meals and lodging is paid for with my Medicaid insurance so I have reassurance. The other inmates have gone mad. If you could just imagine, it's so sad, being tied to a bed. Speaking truthfully, would I eat here and be fed? When will this insurmountable insanity end? When will the post traumatic stress end? When will I be set free to relish in the time spent with family and friends? Please, God, release me from this torch chamber where my body and spirit are burning in Hell. I need to be free so I can tell my family and friends. I am grateful for the compassion of the staff. The endearing social workers console me. Yet, I can't utter a laugh. I work with the doctors and nurses. I would like to lay back and have a mimosa; I could finally rest easy in peace. There is so much more to speak like a thesis. Something in frightening versus. I can't even fathom the shining sun and stars from my hospital bed. The thoughts are lingering like night terrors. I am dead. They gave me an anti-christ pill for psychosis called Ativan. I respectively call the med Out Of It because I feel completely numb like Pink Floyd recites. Pink Floyd was right on track, God, please take me back. I have repented for all of my sins. I am accountable and will apologize. Look into my tie dye colored eyes. Now I am able to release and cry. If this book project makes me a lot of money, I will continue to entertain and be funny. A large portion of my money will go towards charities. My first priority is to end world disease.

*

I am home from the mental institution and I am having night terrors from my episode. I just want to cleanse my mind, body, and spirit. I feel drained, beaten like a dead horse. I have so much remorse. I don't categorize any human who is plagued with mental illness as crazy or insane. They are more a human being plagued with some semblance of a consciousness of demonic possession. To put it candidly, I think people who suffer on the light side are just plain *mashugana* (crazy). Maybe a bowl of chicken matzo ball soup (Jewish penicillin) will cure their ailments instead of all these man made medicines that help the mind, so to speak. The side effects inevitably will damage or kill you. In the first week when I was hospitalized, I couldn't shower. My psychosis was so bad that I absolutely thought that water was the blood of Yeshua during his crucifixion. Not to mention that I was so paranoid and depressed about ending up back in the hospital. I couldn't get out of bed. It felt like I had a ventilator on me and it was code blue. Sophia, being the great provider and parent, would always make me smile. She told me I laid in bed so much that I should do mattress commercials to make some money. All I would need to do was turn in different positions. I begged the higher ups to help me to guide me; to give me strength to come back to the land of living. To give me the strength to function again. I felt like I was lying in an open casket. At least I was still breathing, even is the Earth's air wasn't purified. My soul had been kidnapped and abducted by the evil consciousness. I joked about my many different visits to the psych ward. At least someone knew me by my first name. None of this was a walk in the park or an all-expense paid trip. Perhaps I was just accruing different options for time shares. Between the many suicide attempts and psychiatric hospital, the night terrors would sneak up on me and startle me to the point where I would cry, tremble and shake. Maybe it was best to escape reality. Anyway, everybody's interpretation of what their reality is is different from the man next door. I met some colorful, candid, loving characters this time around and I had struck oil with their presence. I found them to be angelic. Pardon me, let me introduce you to some of the characters.

Paige was a hardcore schizophrenic. He was unkempt with his long beard. He was dirty, non-responsive and yet a very good man. He spoke to himself all day long but perhaps no one has time for anyone else's problems. Perhaps he wouldn't get the response he was looking for. Perhaps he didn't like crowds. He and I would shoot basketballs, trying aimlessly to get the ball in the net. Surely, the New York Knicks weren't going to draft us yet.

Elissa was a twenty-one-year-old mandated to do ECT (electro convulsive shock treatment). I am sure that knowing I was going to a state hospital was enough of a shock. When is it enough?

I speak as one who knows. Over a decade, I did ECT on and off. So to speak, I was more on than off. My memory was greatly affected by the treatment. Maybe these doctors were doing me a big favor. Maybe I was better off not remembering all of the horrific parts. Yet I couldn't remember so many of the happy memories. My friends and family would tell me stories of all the memories we shared. They were so blissful and hilarious. It is such a battle to find that balance. The only balance I can't find is when I check my bank balance that sadly shocks me. I remember days when I was content and peaceful. Knowing I had great wealth and now I bounced checks was hard. They have springs attached to them. At one point, I filed bankruptcy. On the fourth of July, I couldn't afford food even at Burger King, Wendy's or McDonalds. In my past, I would have filet mignon and lobster tails at the finest steak houses. I was more apt to feel like I lived in the land of the free and the home of the brave. Once again, I was barely existing in the pit of fury. Financially broke and that's no joke. Back from riches to rags, nothing to brag about. I wondered if I would ever be well off again but I had doubt. My disability check was less than the money I would make as commission on one deal in my advertising career. But that was ten years previous. Why live in the past, when the future is so peaceful and prosperous?

It was so difficult to make money. I desired to go back to work to feel a purpose again. Yet I could only make $1300 a month on social security or I would lose my benefits. The way I look at it, how can I truly benefit? How could I take the other path and work full time while I would be essentially embezzling money from the government? That would lead to time in jail. So where did that leave me? It left me completely and utterly financially strapped. Thank God, the creator gave me leeway again and my creativity flourished. I had been shut down with a massive clogged artery of my muse's heart for close to three years. The only time I wrote was to sign checks.

Getting back to my stay at the hospital (Hotel California) I was so ill and doubtful about reviving and resurrecting myself. The angelic harp was played over the microphone and each patient's eyes would begin to go from being comatose to having life again. My doctor met with me and asked me if I would consider going to a state hospital for long term care. I told him the only state I would consider would be in the state of New York. It's always better not to feel alone. Yet sometimes, it's astounding to be alone.

It was so heart wrenching when my mom would come visit me in the hospital. I couldn't speak or feel. I was so paranoid of human contact not just because of the Covid 19 virus but, more so that, Satan had me handcuffed to his cage. I knew the Man Upstairs in His renovated co-op would cooperate with me. He would build me an elevator back to the flourishing garden of Eden. After all, I was God's beautiful, pink blooming rose. Sophia reiterated to me that if my father was still alive, he would have given up. I strongly disagreed. But I didn't want to have an escalating argument with

Sophia. She became emotionally abusive due to her pain, fear, and frustration. When you love somebody so deeply and you see them sick and suffering, you suffer with each sword that plays on your heart. The vessel of your own heart's beating stops. With every authentic, deep relationship, you're bound to experience the pinnacle of love and pitfalls of rage. Over a lifetime, I endured much emotional abuse from Sophia. It's not so much that what she was saying was not the truth, it's just that I didn't want to hear it. Sophia was such a classy dame, yet, at times, her delivery of vulgar or hurtful words bordered an uncouth. There were times when Sophia would rage and point her finger in my face like I was a five year old old child that was being sent to time out. In her defense, many times I would want to stick my middle finger in Sophia's face and say, "go fuck yourself and let me know how it works out." Then the matter would escalate, leading to a possible murder so to speak. But I had too much love and respect for Sophia to ever address her with such vengeance.

Allow me to introduce some other characters from my stay at the institution.

Chaz was a thirty-something young, handsome, intelligent man. When I met him, I immediately gravitated to his awesome aura. Chaz loved reading the New Testament and sharing its omnipotent words and actions with other suffering souls. I'll never forget when his sweet mother visited. They were crying in sync and felt so blessed to be reunited. His mother sat on Chaz's lap as they exchanged words of healing and encouragement. I had just come from church and had holy water. I begged her to put some on her forehead to fight off the wickedness of the arch enemy.

Roberta was an older woman, yet had the soul of a small child blissfully dancing and moving. She had such a pleasant way about her. She could befriend anyone. I felt an abundance of gratefulness when I befriended her. Roberta was so interesting. She accomplished and gave her heart so much. What impressed me the most was the heartwarming relationship she had with her son. They were really good to each other. It reminded me how fortunate I was to have a stimulating and blessed relationship with her own parents.

Camilla was a sweet specimen of a lady. When I arrived I was scared of everyone, even when people came on TV. Camilla would bring me her meal trays and coffee while I laid in bed facing the wall and writing 666 with her fingernails. I was so ill that I thought no pill could save me. I was drowning rapidly and needed an abundance of lifeguards. Camilla kept speaking about the same things, repeating them to herself and others. At one point, I mentioned 6,000,000 repeatedly. I knew Camilla knew my secret of being possessed and repressed by Satan. I not only thought I was responsible for the holocaust. I also thought I was responsible for all the terrible diseases in the universe. I felt like Camilla was manipulating my mind by talking in riddles Actually, Satan was in the process of a mind fuck. I started to get suicidal ideation from the guilt and shame. Thank God, I was in the hospital. I was safe from hurting herself.

Melina had energy that was so bubbly and vibrant. Before the hospital, she had been in jail and had to endure being locked up again. She was generous with her talents, attending beauty school. Every morning after the medical tests, they would wake you to do your vital signs. I am now vital. I am breathing and my eyes are opened. It was like Melina set up her own salon in the hallway. She would braid each person's hair. Nostalgically, I felt like I was back in twelfth grade or headed for the Bahamas with my favorite school mates.

No matter how incapacitated or bizarrely any of us were acting, we came together to lean on one another. My boyfriend, Mark, would visit each day. I would repeat to him that I wanted to break up because I was demon possessed and too sick and fragile to be in a relationship. I spoke of how much of a burden I had been. It would be better if he found someone else. Mark wouldn't give up. He visited frequently and would sneak in some of my favorite candy. I knew there was a reason I referred to him as sweetness. My time spent in the hospital was, at first, terrorizing. Yet with the help of her doctor and the help and love from the staff, I was blessed.

While in the hospital, I was so psychotic and condemned that I truly felt I was the devil. I asked that I be seen by a rabbi and priest. I wanted to have an exorcism. But they had stopped doing that in the catholic church a long time ago. As a result of the coronavirus, they were unable to meet with me. However, the hospital sent an amazing chaplain named Van. He was so empathetic and helpful. He would pray over me. Something he said resonated with me. He described a wrestling match between Satan and myself. He said after a long, arduous match, I would always end up on top and Satan would always be the loser.

I had an ingenious, insightful, kind doctor in the hospital. I had dealt with him many years prior when he suggested an injection of an antipsychotic medication once a month. I was all for it as long as it wasn't anti-pasta, antichrist or antisemitic. While in the hospital, I made a decision to stop electro convulsive shock treatment. Although I think it helped to a degree, I felt it did more harm than good. My memory was severely impaired. I thought ECT was barbaric. They would put leads on my head and produce a seizure in my brain. I would get terrible anxiety before my treatment, thinking I was going to die on the table from anesthesia. It was far fetched yet it felt so real. Dr. Han suggested a new miracle medicine that just hit the market called Caplyta. He also changed my other medications. I had come to trust Dr. Han's suggestions. Not to mention, I had a crush on him. Dr. Han was a trendsetter with the fancy shirts he would wear.

The new combination really was helping. But I feared I would become immune to the medication and relapse again. I had been on so many drug combinations in the past that I could be a pharmaceutical rep. The key with medicines is to find the right combination. It's like trying to open a locked door without the key clicking. You will not be able to enter. More and more, I was getting back to myself. The women I grew to love, imperfections and all. My mom and brother were concerned I was getting manic by the mere fact that I was happy, silly, creative, talkative. My doctors, including my therapists, assured my family that I wasn't manic— just so grateful to a higher power to be getting better one day at a time. With this last grueling episode, I had a newfound honor for God and a newfound love and thankfulness for Christ.

With this newfound conviction, I felt like I was connected to God's navigation system. Finally, I would be on the right route. Diverting the stop signs and greasing the spinning tires on pavement. There would be no more potholes. The road would be smooth. No more wrong turns, no more dead ends. I peaked in an innate utopia and euphoria. On my first night home from the hospital I was extremely emotional; crying, pleading to God requesting that I, along with my loved ones, stay happy, healthy, and safe. I wanted them to witness the joyful, all encompassing, healthy and productive years for me. The way I envisioned this was that everyone I adored would be actors and actresses. Even my acquaintances would be extras. I would be the producer and God the Creator and director of this hit Broadway show of life. The sun would be glaring and the birds would be chirping to the point of serenading everyone.

Then the miracle happened. After a long spell of writer's block, the floodgates opened wide and I got a rush of ideas and words. I felt like I was a medium or transcriber from the heavens above. I stayed awake for twenty four hours just writing. That was the birth of my third book and I would see it through to the end. In my past, I would have many ideas and opportunities yet I would give up for fear of rejection and fear of failure. What I had gratefully learned along her journey is that there is no perfectionism. It was merely a delusion and farce. No one was going to steal my thunder or peace of mind. It was too priceless and invaluable. I have had a sense of entitlement since birth. Yet it was more evident than ever. I wanted what I wanted, when I wanted it. It was not only for myself, but for all the rest of humans on the planet. I no longer wanted to be patient nor did I want to still be a mental patient. With my sense of entitlement, I would occasionally be a naughty girl. From time to time, I was prone to a temper tantrum or two. It was then that my loved ones would step in as a babysitter of sorts and they would bring me back down to a righteous level of humility. I wanted my three book volumes to be like a world series. For sure a grand slam. They would be for the salvation of humanity. There was still so much beauty to see. I prayed that my literary words would fall into the right hands and that each individual would do their part and understand. They would put all of their soul and heart into a new, rejuvenated Earth. Little by little, humans would witness and testify to the planet's incredulous worth. The light of God surrounds you. The love of God enfolds you. The power of God protects you. The presence of God watches over you. Wherever you are, God is and all is well.

Love is patient and kind, love does not envy or boast, it is not arrogant or rude. It does not insist on its own way, it is not irritable or resentful. It does not rejoice at wrongdoing but rejoices with the truth. Love bears all things, believes all things, hopes all things, endures all things. (1 Corinthians 13, 4-7)

Charting

Once upon a midnight dreary, I had a flashback to day to day charting by doctors and professionals during my lockdown hospitalization before departing. They just met me and know nothing of history and herstory of pain and it's so disheartening. The worst part is being viewed as insane. Doctor Jeckylnhyde, Doctor Seuss, and Doctor Spock add to the treatment, as well as the defeat of my condition. My hospital stay will be a transition into hypocrisy; of not knowing my history and my only diagnosis or medication. I say this with great reservation and hesitation.

Safety plan triggers
What makes you feel upset, stressed or
dysregulated?

temperate too hot/cold
feeling lonely
being told no.

Early warning signs
How can you tell (by your thoughts, mood, behavior
etc) that a crisis may be developing?

Screaming
Pacing
Yelling
Clenched fist
Racing heart
Isolation
Irritability
Swearing

Coping strategies
What can you do to safely manage your emotions
and behavior?

Listening to music
Going to quiet peaceful places
All types of exercise
Coloring
Drawing

Writing
Praying
Meditating
Talking to your support network

Reminders

These things are important to me and will help keep me balanced and supported.

Family
Friends
Professionals
Spiritual/ theological work
Hobbies
Pets
And pursuing creative endeavors

Bipolar is a chronic, often disabling mental health disorder that makes functioning a war and interacting in society difficult. It can also include psychosis or perceiving reality differently from those around you. The cause of bipolar is not yet known. It is believed to be a result of genetic and biological factors (brain chemistry instructure). Bipolar disorder does run in families and occurs in about one percent of the adult population. By our mental factors, we may have a low mood disorder. These may include: where you grew up, toxins, and infections. Symptoms may include: hallucinations, (seeing or hearing things that are not there), delusions, (false beliefs), disorganized thinking and speech, social withdrawal, severe anxiety, feeling unreal, paranoia, insomnia, trouble thinking or concentrating clearly, depression, feeling suicidal, racing thoughts, promiscuous behavior, recklessness , shopping sprees, delusions of grandeur, and rapidity of ideas.

When to seek medical advice:

Your symptoms are getting worse. Family or

friends express concern over your behavior and ask you to seek help. You feel out of control or like you are being controlled by others. You feel like you want to harm yourself or another. You are unable to care for yourself. There are worsening hallucinations. You might be hearing voices that are telling you to harm yourself or others. You feel worsening depression or anxiety.

Day 1

History of present illness

The patient is a 49 year old woman who took a small overdose of her Latuda and zoloft. She then called her mother and her mom called EMS. She denies any homicidal or suicidal ideation. She was just recently inpatient at another facility. At that time, the patient was hearing voices (command type) telling her that she is the devil and that she has bad intentions. She was brought in after a motor vehicle accident, stabilized, and discharged to a homeless shelter.

Day 2

Reason for referral

The patient was referred for neuropsychological studies by the hospital psychiatrist as part of an effort to identify the level and extent of the patient's cognitive and memory dysfunction. There is a concern about possible brain anoxia, resulting in diminution of her respective cognitive capability and this service is being asked to investigate this more thoroughly through psychometric examination.

Background information

The patient is identified as a 49 year old caucasian female with an extensive past history of bipolar disorder (depresive type) with suicide attempts in her past. Subsequently admitted under suicidal watch. According to the records available, the patient has had many hospitalizations and there is a notation in the chart that she has undergone multiple ECT treatments in the past. The patient also confirms on at least two prior occasions she lost consciousness, stopped breathing, and needed to be intubated and revived. The patient also reports that she was involved in a car accident within the last year, but did not report any loss of consciousness. In addition to her chronic depressive symptoms, the patient notes that she has experienced long standing difficulties with her cognitive status, reporting inability to remember recent and remote access and general incapacity with respect to her basic everyday functioning. She identifies difficulty completing or verbalizing her thoughts with clarity or that she is in a state with perpetual brain fog.

Psycho social history

According to the patient, she denies any history of alcohol and substance abuse. She reports that she was living with her boyfriend until recently and, due to her breakup, took residence with her mother in Kingston. According to the patient, she was a high school graduate who attended two years of college and who was an average student academically. Subsequent to school, she worked as an advertising account executive in White Plains, New York. She chose never to get married nor have children due to complications from her mental illness. She is a previous smoker but claims that she quit smoking on many occasions. She has some difficulty remembering past events. So the time with respect to dates involving prior events is difficult for her to conjure.

Mental status examination

The patient was examined on the unit, ambulating with a walker due to apparent imbalance and some recent falls. The patient was agreeable to meeting with me in the consult patient room. And she participated fully and effortly. Her speech was generally clear and coherent, absent of any dysprosody dysarthria. There was a typical loss of goal phenomenon however, which occurred during her communication. When quiet, she was, at all times, alert. Oriented to person, time, and place, she was able to name the current and past president but could not go beyond that. She had some large difficulty in recalling personal biographical information including deets of important accents in her life and more recent circumstances and they relate more to her recent medical history. Her mood was marked by gross dysphoria and a somber outlook. While she denied any immediate suicidal intentions, she claims that she suffers from thoughts of wishing to die. She denied any current auditory or any visual hallucinations. Her thoughts were generally coherent and absent of any psychotic process. She was able to consistently follow two step commands but had some difficulty with three steps. There were no deficiencies on a confrontational naming exercise. Her praxis gnosis were normal. Motor control via pencil and paper activities was mostly normal. Although she struggled with motor integration control, she answered questions willingly but not productively.

Impression

This is a 49 year old female with notable cognitive deficiencies, the origins in course of which are difficult to establish given the absence of any longitudinal psycho metric comparison and the patient's rather unreliable perspective reporting upon the pattern of her neuro psychological decline. Absent this information, the patient's current test profile was enlightening. Nevertheless, she is clearly deficient in several core areas of her cognitive capability primarily within the intentional executive functioning organizational higher order of reasoning and recent and remote memory domains her speed of information processing and visual motor integration capabilities are also mildly to moderately impaired. In contrast, she shows average functioning on the vocabulary subtest which is considered to be a typical hold test and is reflective of lightly her three morbid cognitive capacity. Overall, given the possibility that the patient suffered some cognitive limitations are permanent and will resist her from ever successfully living on her own. Some measure of regular supervision and assistance will be necessary, perhaps a supervised community living once she is medically or psychiatrically stable.

Examination

Mental status exam: general appearance, cacuasian female who appears older than stated age, unkempt. Behavior: bare eye contact, moderate speech- normal rate, intense tone, loud volume rhythms. Mood: okay, sullen. Affect: blunted. Thought content: no allusions elicited, denied suicidal thoughts ideation intent plane or behavior. Thought process: normal. cognition: alert, intact per interview. Memory:

intact per interview, orientation, time, place, person, and situation.

Day 3

History of present illness, interval history

I saw and evaluated the patient and discussed the plan of care with the multidisciplinary team. I called the patient's mother Sophia Tailor, who also provided history on her hospitalizations and medication treatment. The patient is a 49 year old women with bipolar disorder (depressed type) with a long standing history of hospitlization and suicidal ideation. She has prior trials of multiple medications, including Lithium, Latuda and Invega Sustenna, Abilify, Haloperidol, Neurontin, Zoloft, Clozapine, none of which were effective. She also had electroconvulsive shock treatment therapy for many years, but the patient has declined this for the past several years. The mother gives a history of the patient doing well on Caplyta in the past year but for unclear reason after doing so well, the patient went downhill since that time. On interview the patient is a disheveled woman who appears to have Tardive Dyskinesia movements in her mouth and truncal area. She is superficially present and cooperative but is quite impoverished. With psychomotor retardation, slowness of thinking, effect of flattening, depressed and anxious mood. The patient feels she has no direction in life and regrets losing so much time. The patient denies feeling acutely suicidal while in hospital but does continue to feel worthelss and hopeless that she has not made anything of her life. The patient is denying auditory hallucination. Although she admits to command hallucination in the past. She does have internal thoughts that are derogatory and in nature. She denies recent paranoia or manic or symptomatology; she states, " I just cannot function. My mother has had it with me and my brother has had it with me. I do not know what to do."

Day 4

Examination

49 year old female appears older than stated age, good hygiene with wheelchair assist, speech is soft, regular rate, limited fund of knowledge, good eye contact, mood is less depressed/less anxious thoughts. Appears bewildered at times without paranoia or obvious delusion. Insight and judgment are probable baseline.

Day 5

Reason for treatment, reason for referral

depressed/anxious

Chief complaint

Sarai rudderly got out of bed. When the writer
called to meet for an individual session, she states,
"I have nothing to live for." She rated depression
20 out of 1/10 with 10 being the most severe. She
rated anxiety a 10/10. She denies feelings of anger
but is presently irritable in face of expression and
tone of voice much of the session. Sarai is
disheveled. She declined offer of shower supplies
and assistance but stated, " I'll shower tonight, I
promise." Nursing was made aware that Sarai
stated she would shower this evening. Sarai reports
she is only picking at her meals because the food is
terrible. She states her sleep is poor and, "I'm in an
out of sleep all night." She states her goal is to take
a shower tonight. Sarai engaged in a full session of
chair yoga and a deep breathing building
confidence visualization. She was unable to accept
compliments on the effort she put forth during the

session and responded irritably, " oh what do you mean, I finally got out of bed and did something besides lie in bed all day? " Sarai reports feeling of paranoia and that staff and peers are laughing behind her back.

Day 6

History of present of illness/interval history

Patient was seen and evaluated and planned care was discussed with the team. The patient presented today somewhat better groomed, brighter and more spontaneous, stating she was feeling better. She could not re describe ethos, however. Perhaps having more of a sense of taking care of herself and slightly more energized to be out of her room. She did look better groomed and more spontaneous. The patient expressed no suicidal ideation. She asked about what the plan was and was educated about our concern that she had not previously been feeling better and had been doubting her ability to function. She seemed to understand this.

Day 7

Reason for treatment: depressed, stressed and anxious.

Sarai rudderly agreed to meet the writer for an individual session. She was withdrawn to her room in bed for much of today but rudderly agreed to attempt activity with the writer. Sarai continues to read feelings of depression atenned/tend. She denies feeling anxious or angry. Sarai presented with a flat affect and disheveled appearance. She was dressed in hospital gown and green paper scrub pants. Her hair is increasingly knotted. Writer suggested he may bring in "no more tangles" tomorrow and to have Sarai begin to comb out her hair before it reaches the point of no return. Sarai was receptive to this idea. Sarai reports no issues with appetite but states she feels like she is sleeping too much. Sarai states her goal for today is to find out what discharge plan will be. 49 year old female seen in rounds, case discussed with treatment team. Patient reports feeling less depressed, requesting discharge. However, is aware she has limited discharge placements. Was seen for evaluation, for dementia assessment, was in agreement with a consult, denies any side effects to medication prescribed, invoices being forgetful, eating and sleeping reported as improved since admission.

Day 8

Sarai rated depression a 9/10, anxiety a 9/10. She denies feelings of anger. As writer presented different activity, she stated, "I don't want to, I feel so anxious / depressed that I don't feel like doing anything. I feel like my brain has just stopped working." Sarai was disheveled in appearance and dressed in hospital gowns. She states she did shower and is in hospital gowns because "my clothes are being washed." Sarai allowed writer to apply detangler to her hair and, with encouragement, she did start combing out the knots. She tired and gave up quickly, but did allow writer to complete the task. Sarai selected a total of 5 songs to listen to. She reported enjoying watching videos accompanying songs and was even observed singing along to them softly, Sarai reported no problems with sleep or appetite. She states her goal today was to take a shower and "I did."

Day 9

Writer spoke with the patient's mother Sophia to review the plan of care. Writer provided update on clinical status, medication regimen and discharge planning, and DSS housing (department of social services). Sophia reports she feels the patient is not safe to discharge at this time. She reports she speaks with patient daily and feels the patient is not at baseline, reporting the patient continues to present as depressed, confused at times, and isolative to her room. Sophia is not in agreement of discharge to department of social services at this time. Feels that it would be unsafe due to her current mental state. Sophia strongly advocates that the patient be put back on Caplyta medication. Sophia states the patient was put on that medication on her last hospitalization and, within the few days, showed a remarkable improvement. Sophia states because it is such a new medication, that the hospitals don't always have it on formulary but have obtained it from an outside pharmacy and have given it to her while in hospital. Writer informs Sophia that her concerns and feedback would be brought back to the team. Writer communicated the concerns to the treatment team to those who are in agreement with the need for continued treatment and stabilization.

Day 10

The patient was seen and evaluated and a plan of care was discussed with the multidisciplinary team. I reviewed the neuropsychology assessment consultation note. The patient was found to have neurocognitive deficits in multiple domains, including psychomotor, processing speed, executive functioning, and memory contrasted to a relatively baseline level. Of estimated cognitive functioning, the presumption that the patient sustained some sort of brain injury, perhaps anoxic injury, several months prior. As this seemed to mark decline in her overall functioning. Patient was seen lying in bed today. She was disheveled. When asked to get up slowly, she rose impulsively and began walking, persistent on wanting to go home but she would not know where to go. The patient continues to be dysphoric, bewildered, confused and somewhat agitated. This has been a relatively consistent presentation. Her gait does appear to be improved. Her blood pressure readings intermittently show continued orthostatic hypotension. This may be medication related and or related to poor hydration and nutrition status. The patient continues constant for fall risks and disorganization.

Day 11

Tailor, Sarai

<u>Chief Complaint</u>
<u>History of Present Illness/Interval History</u>
The patient was seen and evaluated and plan of care was discussed with the team.
The patient continues to require constant observation for disorganization and falls.
The patient was slightly better in comport today but immediately asked when she could go home. However, again, the patient stated that she felt confused and not herself. When asked to explain further, the patient admitted that she had been paranoid and was isolating to her room. She stated that she was going to speak with her mother this afternoon but she had not spoken to her in some time. Explained to patient that she appears to be somewhat better but continues to get treatment in the hospital because she is not at her baseline. The patient seemed to understand this on some level. She understood that we are going to have a phone call treatment planning meeting with her mother tomorrow.

Day 12

Reason for Treatment
Reason for Referral: Depressed/Anxious
Chief Complaint:

Sarai was in bed when writer went to meet with her
at 13:40. She readily got out of bed and met with
writer for her individual session. She did not use her
walker and when writer reminded her to, she replied
rather forcefully, "I don't need it." Sarai presented
as more alert, more energetic with increased eye
contact and verbal interaction. She denied feelings
of depression. She rated anxiety a 10/10 and anger a
4/10 at the start of session. She states she is angry
with herself, "because I wasted my life. I don't have
anything. I never did anything with my life."

She tells writer, "I am feeling better and I want to
leave the hospital but I know I don't have anywhere
to go yet." She shared with writer that, prior to this
admission, she had been living with her boyfriend

of 5 years. "But we broke up. It was mutual but now I have nowhere to go."

She denied alcohol use. Today Sarai appeared to have attended to her grooming and hygiene needs, although her hair still looks uncombed. Sarai reports no issues with her appetite. She states she feels as if she is still spending too much time in bed."

Sarai states her goal is, "to get out of here. I don't need to be here anymore."

Sarai completed an almost 30 minute chair yoga session. She worked with good concentration and fair plus attention to detail on a complex coloring sheet of her astrological sign. Writer encouraged her to continue working on picture during tonight's open rec group.

Day 13

Writer met with patient for session and to review treatment plan goals. Sarai presented as more alert, more energetic with increased eye contact and verbal interaction. Sarai is able to articulate her thoughts more clearly. Pt is able to process her increased social isolation while on the unit, reporting that she has been feeling general paranoia and that staying in her room assists her with managing that. Pt reports feeling as if the other patients and staff are watching her, laughing at her, and talking about her which she reports has become increasingly distressing. Sarai verbalizes motivation for discharge and reports plan is to "get out there and get an apartment and look for work." Writer explored with patient steps towards achieving those goals, which patient acknowledges the need for more support and oversight in the community. Sarai was able to process her reported feelings of guilt and shame over MH diagnosis and states that she often does not want to reach out to her mother. As she feels that she has become a "burden" to her family. Pt reports feelings of sadness over losing multiple peers and friends due to her chronic mental health issues and emotional instability. Writer provided Sarai with psychoeducation on CBT skills, including challenging intrusive thoughts. Pt was encouraged to attend therapeutic programming for socialization as well as to gain additional information on coping skills to manage illness.

MH-Mental Health
Pt-patient

Day 14

Reason for Treatment
*Reason for Referral: Depressed/Anxious
*Chief Complaint: Sarai was received in her room
and she was in bed at 10:35. She declined to get out
of bed to meet with writer. So session was
conducted bedside.
Sarai rated depression, "Worse than a 10." She rated
anxiety level the same. Sarai rated feelings of anger
an, "8/10." She tells writer, "I'm angry every day.
I'm angry at myself for not doing things the way
they should have been done. Now I'm in this
predicament. I have nothing. I have no boyfriend. I
have no housing. I have no job, or friends, or
children. I have very little family. My life is a
complete nothing."

Sarai tells writer, "I'm not happy to be alive. I wish
I'd never been born or that I could go to sleep and
not wake up. I'm sorry but that's how I feel."

She tells writer, "I feel like I'm getting worse. I
don't feel like the medications are helping. I don't
even want to get out of bed to take a shower. I have
to take a shower tonight because I promised the
nurse I would."

Day 15

Fall on same level from slipping, tripping, and
stumbling with subsequent striking against
furniture, initial encounter.
Doing better with her day.
Encouraged to use walker.
Discontinued constant observation.
Patient given education about falls risk mitigation.

Major neurocognitive disorder due to another
medical condition.
Patient continues to have moderate neurocognitive
disorder, consistent with depression and dementia.
Will require likely structured level of care
placement.

Depressive episode, adding Wellbutrin to the
regimen.
Continue Cymbalta and Caplyta
Encouraged activation, group participation, and
socialization on the milieu.
Ordered:
Sbsq Hospital Care/Day 25 Minutes

Plan
Fall on same level from slipping, tripping and

stumbling with subsequent striking against furniture, initial encounter

On CO (constant observation), fall risk and disorganization.

Major neurocognitive disorder due to another medical condition

Pt. has a diagnosis of dementia according to neurocognitive testing. Seems a bit clearer today.

Still depressed, paranoid seems a little better. Remains dysphoric and disorganized, but more conversant today.

Will continue current regimen, therapies and med management.

d/c planning. Needs structured living situation.

Ordered:

Sbsq Hospital Care/Day 25 Minutes

Plan

Fall on same level from slipping, tripping and stumbling with subsequent striking against furniture, initial encounter.

At risks for falls due to imbalance and poor judgment, postural instability.

Continues on CO Constant Observation.

Major neurocognitive disorder due to another medical condition.

Has moderate dementia, prognosis poor for improvement.

Depressed and still paranoid, giving the Caplyta more time to work for the patient.
May be modest behavioral improvements but requires much encouragement and reassurance from staff.
Continue to promote engagement in the milieu, self-care re: nutrition and hydration.
The patient will likely require skilled nursing placement.

Day 16

Tailor, Sarai

History of Present Illness/Interval History
Pt. was seen and evaluated and plan of care d/w the team.
She was seen in her room, lying in bed, disheveled and dysphoric.
She was actually considerably more conversant, stating she is very depressed about her life and her situation, not working, being re-hospitalized, losing friends. She feels a burden on her family. At the same time, she is able to appreciate the love of her family and seemed to respond to the encouragement of her mother to make the effort to get better.
She denied feeling suicidal. Said the paranoid ideation is somewhat better.
She remained on CO for disorganization and unsteady, impulsive gait.
She has been compliant with medication.
CO Constant Observation.

Progress Note (Individual/Family/Collateral Documentation)
Writer met with patient for session and to review treatment plan goals. Sarai presents with depressed mood. Remains laying in bed facing away from

writer during session. Pt verbalizes feelings of frustration and hopelessness regarding her continued hospitalization. Pt is irritable, demanding to be discharged immediately. Sarai is not able to participate in discussion related to her safety within the community or plans for treatment moving forward. Pt admits that she is having periods of confusion, stating, "every day I am confused about things from the past but also here on the unit." Pt is unable to provide writer with examples. Pt continues to endorse, reporting she knows that the staff and other patient are laughing at her. Pt reports the remains in bed to avoid "dealing with people." Writer provided supportive counseling and reality based feedback. Writer explored with patient strategies for self care and encouraged Sarai to participate in therapeutic milieu.

Day 17

The patient appears to be still paranoid, dysphoric, treatment refractory.

Her current medication does not seem to be improving her much.

This may be secondary to neurocognitive issues related to brain anoxia.

Her gait appears more stable.

Encourage patient to be up and out of bed.

We will consider trial of another of neuroleptic, including clozapine, because the patient has been refractory to both risperidone and Caplyta.

Ordered:
Sbsq Hospital Care.Day 25 minutes

Day 18

Major neurocognitive disorder due to another medical condition

The patient has treatment-refractory psychosis not responding to Caplyta. Treatment nonresponse may be related to neurocognitive disorder, depression or multiple combined factors. The patient states she has been on clozapine in the past and has not benefited. She has also been on Invega Sustenna.

We will add Invega 3 mg daily to current regiment. Consider cross taper. We will consider reinitiation of clozapine as well.

Encourage patient to activate and participate in the milieu.

Disposition planning ongoing, would recognize need for structured placement post discharge

Day 19

Tailor, Sarai

History of Present Illness/Interval History
Patient seen and examined and plans are discussed with team.

Patient was seen lying in her bed. Continues to be disheveled, withdrawn and having strong ideas of reference. Her gait has been relatively steady. She is interacting. Is eating with others with encouragement. She is depressed and hopeless but is denying current suicidal ideation. She continues to state she wants to leave but has no place to go.

Reason for Treatment
*Reason for Referral: Depressed/Anxious
*Chief Complaint: Sarai presented with a flat/constricted affect, decreased initiative/motivation, slightly irritable mood and poor eye contact. She states again, "I have nothing to live for." She denied any urges to engage in self injurious behaviors.

Sarai rates feelings of depression, anxiety and anger a "10/10" at the start of session. At the end of session, she stated, "I don't feel anything. I have no feelings. I'm detached. I can't do anything. I have no motivation to do anything."

Sarai again tells writer that she is isolating to her room and staying in bed, "because I know the other pts and staff are talking about me, laughing at me behind my back." When writer told her that he had not seen or heard anyone on the unit talking about her, she answered, "they are doing it indirectly." She did not elaborate on what this meant.

Sarai tells writer that she showered last night. Today she was dressed in regular clothing. Her hair appeared very tangled and knotted, possibly d/t the amount of time spent laying in bed. She declined use of detangler and offer of a comb to comb the knots out. "I did it last night."

Sarai states she is "picking" at her food, "because I don't like the food here. It doesn't taste very good." She reports poor sleep and states, "I'm in bed but awake all night. Maybe I drift in and out of sleep." Writer attempted to explain to Sarai that if she were more active during the day, attended groups or strolled the unit, she would expend more energy and possibly sleep better at night. She was unconvinced.

When asked her goal for today, Sarai said in a loud, irritated voice, "I wanna get out of here."

Behavioral Health Notes
Writer attempted to meet with patient for session and to review treatment plan goals. However, Sarai declined to speak with writer. Sarai remains laying in bed, flat affect, engages minimally with writer, answering, "I don't know." Pt denies reports "I don't feel like talking to you right now." Writer will continue to assess patient, build therapeutic rapport.

Day 20

Writer spoke with patient's mother Sophia and provided update on mental status, medication regimen, and plan of care. Writer informed mother regarding plan to refer patient to skilled nursing facility for increased support and supervision. Sarai verbalizes agreement with plan and thanked writer for the assistance.

Day 21

Treatment team held conference call with patient's mother Sophia to review plan of care and provide update on clinical status. Team provided update on current medication regimen, SPOA housing screening, and current mental status. Sophia reports she is concerned that the patient is still not returning her calls and she feels the patient is becoming more confused and disoriented. Sophia reports the patient called her the previous evening asking concerning questions which she already has the answers to. Such as, "how many children does my brother have?" and "where are you living?" Patient thought brother had children and was keeping them from her because she was mentally ill. Believed mother was living on a beach in Florida. Team explored with the patient her treatment goals and needs to stay safe within the community. Pt continues to focus on immediate discharge and is not able to articulate any progress made towards treatment goals or how she would care for self while in the community. Pt remains isolated to her room and pt was encouraged to take an active role in her treatment while in the hospital, including attending treatment groups and attending to ADL's (activities of daily living). Sophia thanked writer for update and reported no additional questions.

Day 22

Reason for Treatment
*Reason for Referral: Depressed/Anxious
*Chief Complaint: Sarai presents as depressed and irritable. She made poor eye contact and looked past writer rather than at him. She reports feeling paranoid and states, "I know people on the unit are talking about me and laughing at me." Sarai rated depression, anxiety and anger a "10/10" and then added "It's beyond that really. I just want to be left alone."

When writer asked Sarai if she felt suicidal, she responded, "my life is already over. I have nothing to live for."

She tells writer, "the meds aren't helping me."

Sarai states she has no support system and she is unable to identify any positive coping skills, leisure activities, or hobbies she enjoys.

Sarai was resistant to attempting therapeutic activities and became increasingly irritated the more the writer encouraged her to participate. Sarai remained in supine position in bed and refused to even sit. She made superficial attempts at deep breathing exercises and half-heartedly attempted some stretches but with no energy or enthusiasm.

She reports, "eating a little bit, not a lot because I hate the food here." She reports poor sleep and states, "I'm up all night long." Writer encouraged Sarai to engage in activities during the day to help expend energy and increase feelings of tiredness as bedtime approaches. But she stated, "no, I don't want to."

Day 23

Reason for Treatment
*Reason for Referral: Depressed/Anxious
*Chief Complaint: Sarai is becoming increasingly more difficult to engage in activities. She is most often received laying in bed on her side facing toward the window. She is consistently making much less eye contact and her verbal responses are becoming more terse and guarded. She refused writer's encouragement this morning to get up and to take a shower. Writer offered to gather shower materials for her and to escort her to shower room and stand outside door is her were feeling paranoid. Her response was, "no. That's OK. I don't want to." She refused encouragement to sit, apply hair detangler and comb the knots out of her hair. Sarai continues to rate depression, anxiety, and anger a "10/10." She is unable to identify any reasons to live and states, "my life is over." She is unable to identify any positive, life affirming actions she can take to keep self safe if actively suicidal and states, "nothing."
She reports poor appetite. "I don't like the food here" and she states her sleep is, "terrible." Writer pointed out that if she were more active during the day and spent some time out of bed and engaged in activities she might sleep better when nightime rolls

around. Sarai's response was to shrug and state, "I don't feel like doing anything."
She half-heartedly engaged in a few stretches. When given max verbal encouragement, while laying in bed (she declined to select the type of music she would like to have on) and engaged in a one minute breathing meditation. She did verbalize, "that was nice." But declined to do any more than that.

When she was asked what her goal is for today, she stated, "I don't have one."

Day 24

Reason for Treatment
*Reason for Referral: Depressed/Anxious
*Chief Complaint: Sarai presented increasingly
alert and energetic than in past visits. She also
presented as more irritable. When writer
complimented her and told her she looked well, she
responded, "oh yeah, right, I'm not falling for that
one." She rated feelings of depression and anger a
"10/10." But denied feelings of anxiety. Sarai
reports that she has been keeping herself busy, "by
reading. I have some good books that my roommate
gave me." Sarai agreed to attempt a deep
breathing/relaxation meditation with writer and
worked with fair concentration. She stated, "That
was nice, I liked that" when it was over. Sarai
almost engaged in an exercise routine using 3lb
weights. But just as we were about to begin, she
stated, "nevermind, I changed my mind. I'd rather

just read. Do you think you could find some more books for me?"

Sarai showered this a.m. and was dressed in her regular clothing and eye glasses. Her hair looked at least part way combed out.

Sarai reported no issues with appetite or sleep and said, "it's okay."

She identified her goal for today as, "to read and relax."

Day 25

*Chief Complaint: Sarai was visible walking in the milieu. She readily agreed to meet with writer for individual session. She made fair minus to fair eye contact and expressed appreciation for romance novel that writer brought over for her. Sarai's affect is generally constricted and she has flashes of irritability when writer asks her questions. But overall, she was cooperative and attempted all activities presented to her.

Sarai rated feelings of depression a "5/10" She denied anxiety and anger.

Sarai knew the month and year and that she is in hospital
She was a little off on the day and thought it was Thursday. Writer informed her that the dry erase board usually has the day, month, and year written on it along with the groups being offered for the day and she replied, "Thanks, I'll check it out." Sarai appears to be attending more consistently to her ADL's. She was dressed in regular and clean clothes and it looks as if she brushed her hair. Sarai states her goal for today is, "to go to groups."

Day 26

Reason for Treatment
*Reason for Referral: Depressed/Anxious
*Chief Complaint: Sarai was received in her room where she was found laying in bed reading. She is dressed in her regular clothing and informs writer she showered and used deodorant today. Her hair looked as if she had at least attempted to comb it.

Sarai readily agreed to get out of bed and accompany writer to a group room to engage in individual session. Sarai was polite but guarded, with many of her responses being clipped and curt.

She reported continued feelings of paranoia and the feeling staff and peers are talking about her. She rated intensity of paranoia a "7-8/10"

At the start of session, Sarai rated depression, anxiety, and anger a "10/10" She verbalizes feeling frustrated about continued hospitalization and states, "I just want to be discharged. There is nothing for me to do here."

By end of session, Sarai rated depression and anxiety a "7/10" and anger/frustration an "8/10"

Sarai reports she is eating 3 meals/day, "even though I don't really like the food here." Tells writer, "I don't really sleep. I just kind of chill out all night long."

Sarai states her goal today is, "to go to some groups." She thanked writer at end of session, saying, with a very light smile, "thank you, for meeting with me."

Day 30

Reason for Treatment

*Reason for Referral: Depressed/Anxious

*Chief Complaint: Sarai was initially irritable and annoyed when writer went to her room to meet with her for individual session. She stated, quite loudly, "I don't want to do anything today!" Writer reminded her that, over the weekend, she had inquired about receiving materials to move excess and unwanted facial hair. Sarai replied, "oh yeah. You can help me with that?"

Writer had Sarai select a musical artist she wanted to listen to while she engaged in ADL activity and her mood seemed to soften. She hummed and sang along at times softly.

Sarai worked with good concentration and good attention to detail on tweezing activity. She expressed displeasure with the quality of the tweezer and, to be fair, it has seen better days. Sarai was appreciative when writer told her he would have a better one for her tomorrow. Sarai tweezed the majority of her neck and chin. She decided to wait until tomorrow to do her upper lip and other areas. Sarai engaged in an aromatherapy activity and stated she found the scent of lavender, "very nice, relaxing." Sarai rated feelings of depression,

anxiety and anger an "8/10. You know the usual."
Sarai stated her goal for today is, "you know, if they
have groups to try to go to some. Even though I
don't really like being around a lot of people."

Sarai made no mention this morning about feeling
evil or being possessed by the Devil.

Day 31

Reason for Treatment
*Reason for Referral: Depressed/Anxious
*Chief Complaint: This afternoon at 13:30, Sarai was found in room and in bed. She expressed gratitude that writer had come back to see her so she could continue using tweezers to remove unwanted facial hair. Sarai worked with good concentration and good attention to detail on this task. It is taking time because, over the course of her stay, she has acquired quite a bit of facial hair. Sarai shared with writer, "if I were home, I would have just waxed my face but we can't do that here."

Sarai rated depression and anxiety a "7/10." She denied feelings of anger. Sarai is still reporting paranoid thoughts and feelings and the belief that staff and peers are talking about her behind her back. She did not identify any specific people she believed this of. Sarai stated her goal is to attend a group and we reviwed today's group schedule on the dry erase board. Sarai's hair was matted and tangled but she declined offer of detangler and a comb.

While working on activity, Sarai selected musical artist Billy Joel to listen to and sing along to. Sarai again expressed appreciation for opportunity to attend to her appearance when session was done. Plans were made to meet again tomorrow so that Sarai could complete this grooming task.

Day 33

Reason for Treatment

*Reason for Referral: Depressed/Anxious

*Chief Complaint: Writer met briefly with Sarai to see that she had settled into her new environment and to help orient her to the unit. Sarai tells writer, "I like it over here. It's bigger over here. I have more room to walk around. I have my own shower. I like that. I also have a better view over here."

Writer showed Sarai where the dry erase board is where the daily groups are written down and where the rooms are where groups are held. Writer asked Sarai if she had any questions and she did not. We ended session with a brief deep breathing meditation. Sarai was calm and unagitated. The entire time we met was approximately 15 minutes.

Progress Note (Individual/Family/Collateral Documentation)

Writer met with patient for session and to review treatment plan goals, which patient verbalizes agreement with. Pt presents as irritable, anxious and remains laying in bed during session. Writer reviewed recent events which led to switch to another unit. Pt explains that she felt another patient and the staff were laughing at her, talking about her, and calling her names. Writer provided reality testing and explored with patient strategies to communicate her needs/frustrations. Pt reports feeling consistent paranoid regarding other patients and staff. However, shows some insight that the peer and staff may not have been targeting her. Pt verbalizes frustration over continued hospitalization, reporting feelings of hopelessness, passivity, stating, "I don't want to actively kill myself, I just don't see any will to live."

Writer provided supportive counseling and encouraged patient to utilize self soothing techniques such as coloring and reading.

Day 36

Reason for Treatment
*Reason for Referral: Depressed/Anxious
*Chief Complaint: Sarai presented as eager to meet for her individual session. She initiated request for session by stating, "let's do some coloring and listening to music today." Sarai also engaged in an aromatherapy activity and a chair yoga set of exercises.

At the start of session, Sarai rated depression, anxiety, and anger a "6/10." By the end of session, she rated all three emotions a "4/10" She was able to state, "the lavender (oil), the music, and the stretching was very relaxing. Thank you."

Sarai was able to identify the two reasons she would like to continue living are, "maybe go back to school and exercise my mind" and "try to enjoy my life a little more."

Sarai identified "tell someone" as a positive action she could take if felt suicidal in the future.

Sarai worked with fair plus concentration and attention span on all activities. She expressed enjoyment and thanked writer, "for coming down and getting me out of my room."

Sarai stated she did attend a group yesterday and that her goal today is to attend another one.

Sarai reports she is showering. She is dressed in regular clothes but her hair remains uncombed. She declined offer of detangler and a comb.

Day 41

Progress Note (Individual/Family/Collateral Documentation)
Writer met with patient for session and to review treatment plan goals, which patient verbalizes agreement with. Pt is witnessed to be sitting up in bed, improved grooming, reading a book. Pt's affect is brighter, eye contact is appropriate. Pt reports improved mood and is able to articulate herself more clearly and coherently. Pt reports she continues to feel paranoia however she is now able to "check myself" and start to challenge paranoid thoughts. Pt is witnessed to be more visible on unit and has shown increased participation in therapeutic milieu. Writer praised patient and encouraged her to continue to participate in therapeutic programming. Writer reviewed with patient strategies to manage anxiety/paranoia when in social settings and encouraged pt to take small breaks in her room to regroup if needed. Pt thanked writer and agreed, "that is my goal."

Day 43

Progress Note (Individual/Family/Collateral Documentation)
Writer met with patient for session and to review treatment goals, which patient verbalizes agreement with. Pt presents with slightly pressured speech. Pt is witnessed to be socializing with peers. Pt reports improved mood, affect is bright, uses humor with writer appropriately. Pt reports concerns related to her recent weight gain and states plan to stop taking her medication, as she believes this is cause for her weight gain. Writer provided psychoeducation on her current medication regimen, reminded her that her mood/thought clarity has improved because of her medications and encouraged her to speak with the MD related to any specific medication questions. Writer provided psychoeducation to pt regarding healthy eating habits and exercise, encouraged patient to participate in movement groups. Pt was receptive and reports she will connect with the doctor regarding her medication questions.

Day 52

Called to see patient after she was assaulted by her roommate. Patient states she was punched several times on left upper arm without provocation. She complains of pain and states several times that she is anxious and traumatized. She was not struck in the head. Only on the arm. She was worried that her roommate was going to attack her again when she was sleeping, but she was transferred

O. NAD
Head-ncat
Neck-supple
Ext-LUE-no ecchymosis, no abrasion, no swelling.+tenderness to palpation lat aspect upper arm.ROM-wnl wrist, elbow,shoulder

Neuro-motor5/5
A.Contusion left upper arm
P.Ice/tylenol.motrin prn
Follow up if increased pain

Day 53

*Chief Complaint: Sarai presented as extremely happy to see writer (who has been away for the past two weeks.) Sarai stated, "are you amazed by my resurrection? I feel so much better. I'm not half dead any more." Sarai presented with rapid, pressured, and loud speech. Her mood was labile, elated but easily irritated. She presented as eager to engage in individual session but needed moderate refocusing at first to stay involved in activities because she was very easily distracted. Sarai presented as grandiose. She tells writer, "I've written 3 books since you've been gone and I'm going to self publish them. I'm also going to open a treatment facility one day. I've already asked some of the staff to work there. I'd like you and your wife, the social worker. to work there also. I'll talk to you more about it as I get closer to discharge." Sarai denied feelings of paranoia. She states, "I don't think the Devil is possessing me anymore. I don't think the Devil is after me. I don't think people are talking behind my back anymore."

Sarai denied feelings of depression, anxiety or anger. She states, "I feel great."

Day 54

The patient was evaluated this morning. Chart, labs, and medications are reviewed. The patient is observed in the dining hall eating breakfast with peers and denies any changes in her appetite. Her mood is anxious with congruent affect. Patient reports that peers on the unit have "disrespected me. I'm not standing for that. I just want to be discharged. I need to be discharged." She reports sleeping "okay" last evening and continues to remain in behavioral control at this time. The patient states, "I have received excellent care, Dr., I want to know who you report to. The CEO needs to know of your rude behavior." Patient requesting Ativan for anxiety PRN. She is provided extensive education pertaining to prescribed medications. She continues to attend therapeutic groups to enhance her coping mechanisms. She remains social with select peers and staff. She continues to consistently deny self injurious behaviors. She verbalizes needs/concerns appropriately to staff. Patient is encouraged to comply with medications, maintain good behavioral control, attend therapeutic groups, and to attend to personal hygiene. Patient verbalizes understanding and patient is agreeable to treatment plan. We will continue to provide encouragement, support, psychoeducation pertaining to medications and therapies. We will continue discharge planning as clinically indicated by patient's response to treatment and medication stabilization as she progresses to her baseline. We will continue to pursue appropriate housing to the Assisted Living for the patient to facilitate safe discharge planning.

Day 55

Progress Note (Individual/Family/Collateral Documentation)
Writer met with patient for session and to review treatment plan goals, which patient verbalizes agreement with. Pt present with slightly elevated mood, lightly pressured speech. Pt is more visible on unit. Pt verbalizes some grandiose, delusional ideation, reporting that she is publishing a book while in the hospital which describes her experience in the hospital and that she is in the process of creating a non profit organization in which writer will be granted a directorship position. Writer processed with patient previous physical attack that patient experienced by peer. Pt reports feeling traumatized, reporting that the peer's "explosive anger frightened me greatly." Writer provided supportive counseling, reality based feedback, and explored positive coping skills to continue to manage intrusive thoughts. Pt verbalizes frustrations related to continued hospitalization and demands immediate discharge. Writer validated feelings, processed with patient the feedback from the Assisted Living placement option and encouraged patient to use self soothing strategies.

Occupational Therapy Forms

Sarai identified, "I stop taking care of myself and my appearance. I get really withdrawn and quiet. I become really unfocused and disorganized" as early warning signs that she needs to attend to her mental health needs.

Sarai identifies, "reach out to my family and friends" and "be honest about what I'm thinking and feeling" as positive actions she can take to keep herself safe if feeling suicidal.

Sarai identifies, "writing and singing" as positive coping skills. She also added "doing the yoga and meditation you taught me."

Sarai reports she is sleeping and eating well. Sarai states her goal is, "stay well no matter how much hard work it takes."

Day 56

The patient was evaluated this morning. Chart, labs, and medications were reviewed. The patient presents as cooperative and remains hyperverbal and elevated. The patient states, "I'm hypomanic, not manic. However, I will entertain you with my jokes....United we stand, divided we fall. What do you ask a maintenance man? Ask him if he screws." She exhibits tangential thinking and histrionic behaviors. Her mood is elevated, with congruent affect. She reports sleeping poorly on the unit. Requests increase in melatonin, refusing to accept Trazodone at bedtime. She denies any changes to her appetite. Her eye contact is good. She has been accepting all medications as prescribed with the exception of her Trazodone and denies any potential side effects related to the medications. She reports feeling "very good. I'll tell you a joke and you'll pour me a Coke." She has been attending therapeutic groups to enhance her coping mechanisms. She remains social with staff and peers alike. She continues to consistently deny and self injurious behaviors at this time. The patient is visible on the unit and can verbalize needs/concerns appropriately to staff. Patient is encouraged to comply with medications, maintain good behavioral control, attend therapeutic groups, and to attend to personal hygiene. Patient verbalizes understanding and patient is agreeable to treatment plan. We will continue to provide encouragement, support, psychoeducation pertaining to medication and therapies. We will continue discharge planning as clinically indicated by patient's response to treatment and medication stabilization as she progresses to her baseline. We will continue to pursue appropriate housing for the patient.

Day 57

History of Presenting Illness/Interval History
Patient seen and evaluated. Patient reports "good" mood and denies any irritability. She reports sleeping "well" last night. 7 hours after she was started on Melatonin. Her mood is slightly elevated and is inquisitive, which appears to be her baseline. She reports good appetite. Denies any problems with energy. She denies suicidal ideation/homicidal ideation intent or plans. States that, "I will never do it again, I have suffered indurably." She is adherent with medications and denies any side effects. Treatment team is working on stable housing for the patient.

Redeem the Dream 33 (Heaven)

Volume Two

By Ms. Lori Eve Tatarsky
aka Sarai London Tailor

Redeem the Dream 33
(Heaven)

The pen is mightier than the sword? The sword
needs blood, erosion and chaos. Whereas the pen
creates power by example, fierce strength, and the
possibility of enduring love. The notion is
conclusive that the sword shall never conquer or
bring upon pain to the penetrable pen.

Awakenings

1992-1993

I never quite understood why they called it the "funny farm." In retrospect, I smile and remember it as a slapstick episode of Benny Hill. But at twenty one years old, it felt like blood loss from an open wound—the disappearance of certainty into the veil of panic.

When you're young, people don't tell you to adapt; to remove the mask of innocence before awakening into harsh reality.

My journey through life became infested with detours. My straight and narrow path became cluttered with the debris of jagged turns and my soul became magnetically drawn to a dark, bottomless pit. The only concrete thing I could focus on was that the road I was traveling upon would lead me somewhere. To be quite honest, I felt secure in my interpretation. At least I knew this would lead me to a place, even if it was to a halting dead end.

I could only make the journey from what I was to what I could be by moving through the present. That journey could only be made when I was willing to go to any lengths to find true happiness. Once I had this revolutionary awakening, I was confident that the place I was heading for would have just as much power as the place I had come from.

I relished in the wonder of playing the role of the fairy princess. Everything felt so mystical and magical. The stage on which I acted had an omnipotent power with no trace of a closing curtain.

I loved my father. He was the world to me, he was the very rock of seven continents. All the storybooks in the world were not needed. Then he got terminally sick and, at only forty seven years old, he passed because he was a hard working family man who suffered a heart attack. The imagery, the drama, of my childhood faded. All the rhythm became a background drone and, as he got sicker, so did I. Not even the waving of my wand could save either of us.

For the first time in my life, material things were meaningless. Childhood was shattering—I had absurd questions. In his time of need, it felt like I was abandoning him, but wondered if he had abandoned me.

I anticipated reading the next pages of my storybook family. Each page left me hanging on; wanting to acquire more of this perfect picture I had created in my disillusioned mind. Too much of a good thing must come to an end. How true that statement was, because as time unfolded the pages of the book became shorter and the words became intensely blurred.

When I reached this destination, I didn't feel the self doubt. I didn't fear the unknown and I certainly wasn't caught up in my chaos. Yet, I mercifully wanted to heal my bruised soul. I achingly needed to refuel my empty heart. I mournfully grieved the loss of the gleam in my eyes and the vivacious energy behind my smile. So for the first time, I was willing to take an about face and stare back to the starting point of this exhausting and precarious road.

It was an amazing paradox. It was a miraculous new beginning. It was a journey back to the Creator and the childlike individual; the one I had lost and so unconditionally loved.

Eulogy

January 11, 1989

My Beloved FATHER,

There are two kinds of people in this world. There are quitters...the ones who give up because it's convenient and a lot easier to give up and there are the fighters...the ones that fight and continue to fight...not always winning—but at least making an attempt.

If I ever knew a fighter and a champion, it was YOU. BLAKE TAILOR was a man who did and gave everything for his family. There was much love in this man... He didn't always come out and say what was in his mind but one could always feel this love from his sense of humor.

His sense of humor was the one unique thing I will cherish and remember my Father for. When my Father became ill, I didn't want to accept what was happening. I couldn't understand why it had to be my family that had to suffer. I tried to block it out and run away from the situation; not because I did not love him but because I loved him so much that I couldn't stand to see him in so much pain and so very helpless.

When you passed away yesterday, I was totally destroyed. Especially since it was my birthday and that day was always supposed to be happy for me. Yet, as I thought about it, I realized that your pain and suffering had ended and you are now finally at peace...and that is the best present I can ever receive.

YOU have left us for the time being, but I know you...OL' BLUE EYES #2 WILL ALWAYS BE LOOKING DOWN ON US, JOKING WITH US, GUIDING US, AND LOVING US.

Throughout this long and treacherous route, I have never seen a woman more courageous and loving than my mother. She was far more than a Florence Nightingale...She was a savior for my brother and myself. I don't think that there is a person in the whole world that I have more love and respect for than this WOMAN—my mother. She is one of a kind.

The worst of this nightmare is over and in time we will all go on.

We are a strong bunch. We got that from our father.

I think that the best way my father would like to be remembered is by saying: REGRETS, HE HAD A FEW...but too few to mention. He did what he had to do and saw it through without exception, but much more than this...HE DID IT HIS WAY...

MY BELOVED FATHER, MOMMY, GARRETT AND I WILL LOVE YOU NOW AND FOREVER

AND UNTIL WE MEET AGAIN!

The Yellow Hooded Madagascar

A Compilation of Vignettes
(Literary Essays & Poetry)

The Yellow Hooded
Madagascar

Daddy's Little Princess

I have nowhere to run.

I have nowhere to hide.

There is a toxic secret.

A death sentence: AIDS

Locked up inside.

I feel like a wild gorilla in a cage.

Why can't I speak my truth?

I have so much rage.

It festers inside me and destroys my veins.

I feel all alone; I feel insane.

I deserve to have my say.

I'll throw myself, knees first, on the ground and

      pray.

Wanting to regain everything past,

Hidden, huddled, on this stage of sorrow, aghast;

I search endlessly for answers. So, how am I to
    feel?
Isn't life supposed to be
One bottomless bowl of cherries?

Then why do I feel like
I've inhaled the pits?
My dancing, twirling heart feels
Torn from within;
Concluding it must have given quits.

Clinging Dreams

1992

All I want to do is protest
And arrest this reality and finality of death.
My daddy will no longer have breath.

On my knees to pray.
This wish of mine,
To turn back time to the happy from this gray.

How does the predicament of the
challenging Game of Life really work?
Is it simultaneous that when you
Are truly content,
Fatalistic travesties must somewhere lurk?

I never fathomed,
Not even in my most
Horrifying state
Of the reality that has become.
I have nowhere to hide.

I have nowhere to run.

At the end of the rainbow,

There lies my pot of gold.

Will it ever be mine,

Now that my soul was sold?

I was forever being controlled,

No better off than a puppet-like toy.

I was used, abused, and confused.

Boy, were they manipulative and coy!

I was placed high on a rising pedestal,

Only to be pushed and pulled at, to fall.

I was the Belle of the Ball.

So, who am I now?

I have widely opened my eyes.

I'm a person that's a little less helpless,

Far more wise.

The fairy tale has ceased.

The nightmare has just begun.

A chilling, icy reality blocks the setting of the sun.

The cave's long dark cannot blind, break, or burden.

And even in this new found freedom,

Awareness of lost innocence,

The pot of gold I shall find.

The Yellow Hooded Madagascar

1993

Somebody once told me the story of the
Yellow Hooded Madagascar: a bird so entrancing
that when it would fly into town once a year, all the
villagers would gather together to hear it. The long-
beaked traveling bird's spring song was so uniquely
spellbinding, that both commoners and elites would
drop what they were doing just to hear the clarion
call. For hours, onlookers would not—could not—
move; swallowed in the beauty of the bird's lyrical
musings.

I wondered if it was a bird of my feather. I
wondered about its origin. Yet as time unfolded and
I researched this matter, I found it to be a huge
fallacy.

The truth that I had believed was, indeed,
not the truth at all. At my worst times of
vulnerability, insecurity, and weakness, I have not
been able to discern what is real and what is fiction.

The Yellow Hooded Madagascar does not exist. There is no such bird of my kinship.

The year was 1993 and all was crumbling in my inner world as well as the outer Terra Firma. I was visiting friends at college in Towson, Maryland. I was certainly a lost soul at this juncture. I felt as if I would never amount to anything. I felt as if I had failed my loved ones and my Creator.

I made a conscious, or perhaps subconscious, decision to ingest a tab of LSD. It was then that I would become acquainted with a world of insanity. A firm handshake of "hello, I am now defined as Bi-Polar, who might you be?"

I attempted to get home to Long Island. I needed to find a safe haven. I needed to find a place where I could be protected from the lunacy in my mind.

"Oh, please, God," I prayed, "let me make it to Home Sweet Home."

I drove erratically on the highways, pushing a hundred twenty miles per hour in my Mazda RX-

7; rotary engine screeching. When I reached the Throgs Neck Bridge, it no longer connected me. It had become a green frog's neck with blisters and boils on it. At last, I made it home. Yet, it was anything but sweet.

My mind was not my own and I knew it would just be a matter of time before the Devil was dancing along at my bedside. I heard voices in my whirling mind. The voices instructed me to kill myself. I was utterly stressed, repressed and becoming one with the Dark Side. I believed with every ounce of my being that I was possessed by Satan. His demonic insistence that I take my own life was my induction into the world of mental illness, Devastating, labyrinthine, overtakingly, shakingly vivid.

I was hospitalized and diagnosed with Manic-Depressive Disorder, better known as Bipolar. I had mood swings: highs and lows, ebbs and flows, sometimes coupled with hallucinations. Some other symptoms included catatonic states, delusions of grandeur, spending sprees, rapid

speech, religious delusions, and suicide missions—
to name a few.

My poor mother was first a witness to the
atrocity of the AIDS virus and now her only
daughter was mentally ill in this lifelong odyssey. I
lay in a hospital bed, pulverized by treacherous and
demonic thoughts. My dear mother would visit each
day. She would paint my nails and brush my ratty
hair. Her friend would recite the Lord's Prayer to
me.

What resonated with me most was the line:
"lead us not into temptation but deliver us from
evil." I did not speak to another soul. I feared the
human race. I feared my own shadow. Now I would
be labeled a mentally ill person. Perhaps they would
associate me with murderers, pedophiles, and
thieves. My dreams of a happy, healthy, productive
life vanished. It was a loss of choices, dreams, and
hopes. I felt like damaged goods. I felt as if I would
be placed on a clearance rack.

I was put on high doses of medications and,
slowly, I came back. The entrapping night terrors

began to dissipate. My thoughts returned to lucidity. My mood was elevated to a baseline. The only downside was the numerous side effects: tiredness, tremors, a ferocious appetite, blurred vision, stiff joints. In order to salvage my sanity, I would have to endure these nuisances. It seemed to be a trade off: good versus evil. And I didn't know which brought greater distress.

Upon discharge, my mother welcomed me home. I had realized that, as the immortal phoenix rises from the ashes of death and destruction, I too had been resurrected. Would this resurrection of brightness last or would I continuously return to the

Dark Side? Would I ever have to face the eye of the storm again?

Toddler's Toys in a Gift Box

1995

When you're a child, even the simplest discovery satisfies all daily wants. Until the next day when the thirst for adventure is renewed. They say that the world is your playground. As a young girl, I had envisioned such endless fields of promise. The spotlight of childhood—that adoration, that glitz and glamor—those around me encouraging my every move as fine theater. It left my body with a warm tingle and my mind shining with a boundless sparkle. As I grew up against my own free will, I desired to remain a child desperately, endlessly playing. It was at this devastating point of reality that all of my dreams became earth-shattering nightmares. It became tedious to catch any of my stars; not even the one that gleamed with such an intense and promising spiritual light. So, in the final bouts of my insanity, I had a wondrous awakening of acceptance. I realized that my dreams were far too precious to drift away in the violence of a wind storm. I remember being a child, running exuberantly in my playground. Free-falling down the slide, periodically feeling discomfort from my body hitting concrete. I would immediately release a blood-curdling scream. My darling and precious Mommy would rescue me. She would wipe all of my running tears and caress me until my trembling ceased. I could sprint right back to the top of the slide and begin all over again.

As far as the see-saw went, I never quite liked the fact that I needed another playmate to help balance out all of the ups and downs. Without another child, I was sure to hit either a rock bottom or a high bottom. When I came into recovery, due to the dysfunction of my family origins, I once again needed a playmate to help find equilibrium on the see-saw. This would enable me to monitor the highs and lows and cope with life on life's terms. However, this time I didn't need to look elsewhere for my playmate. All I needed to do was search within for the special child I had detached from so long ago.

One process at a time, I began to feel my inner child's overwhelming energy and, congruently, my adult energy could float symbolically, like the rippling of a calm ocean. As a little girl, I would spin on the merry-go-round. As a young adult, I would portray a gerbil, spinning in a cage on a one-way wheel. I would become so dizzy and confused that I couldn't even begin to fathom who I was any more. I had scattered and racing thoughts, leading to traumatizing depreciation of my soul. Similar to the young tyke who has far too much candy or rocky road ice cream, spinning until they collapse from exhaustion or possibly regurgitating. I always felt an awesome connection with the swings. Perhaps on them, I could experience my flight of fantasy. I embarked over the bird's nest in the swaying branches of the embedded trees. I was mystified by the magical kite that would soar to amazing heights, yet always remained in reach of my small and tender grip.

I always despised the monkey bars. I could never get from one bar to another, so I would purposely drop to the ground. As a little girl, I intuitively sensed that each bar would represent the hardening hearts and tragic events that would occur in our struggling universe. Even in all of my yesterdays, I feared the constant reality of terminal disease, unpredicted traumas, the mask-wearing hoax of humans, and the pointless wars—concluding that all of this was in some way a horrid massacre. Self-preserved souls were destroyed, innocent people lay still in zippered body bags. Human beings dumped underneath rows of dirt. Justifiable endings by the protagonists that would place bouquets of flowers on the burial sites of the tormented victims.

While living in all my self-defeating behaviors and my charades, I was no more alive than the victims. I had become my most lethal, endangered critic. A dominating, black cloud hung over my head and I always knew when to pull the lever that would bestow venomous raindrops of acid on my tired, volcanic mind.

I needed achingly to rid myself of this. For the more I remained focused on it, the colder and blacker my insides grew. Any hopes of clinging onto the fantabulous, fuchsia cloud I had envisioned slowly vanished.

So, I had to start from square one. But miraculously, with each baby step that I dared to take, the black cloud began to metamorphose into an aura of vibrant colors. I was no longer existing in the wrath of Hell. Blissfully, in my blossoming rebirth, I could play in the splendid unwrapping of my gift box. I could play my assigned role with a little less anxiety. Most importantly, with the willingness in both my mind and heart to learn, change and to grow, I could ultimately continue to travel on my allotted journey.

Tatarsky 33:44

You must possess and repossess the sacred heart of a child; the astounding inquisitiveness, cleverness, boundless energy, laughter, and imagination to return to the glorious Kingdom of Heaven. To live life through the eyes of a child with pure and utter magic. Under these parameters and conditions, there will be an open door policy--no questions asked. Never fall prey to this quest. It is undoubtedly the best of the best; la creme de la creme.

It's Showtime

1995

Remove the costume and mask

Need not pretend

Do I know you

You look familiar to me

There is so much beauty

Within us and outside to see

The eyes are the windows to the soul

It is my responsibility to be an example and
      accomplish goals

Some days I am like a wind up doll

Other days I feel utterly dead and removed from
      humanity

I never again as long as I breathe want this to be

I want to soar like the bald eagle

Fly to the dazzling stars

Each moment in time

I want to find a respite and heal

My spiritual and sadistic scars

Glori

Crash Landing

1995

Paradoxical Destruction

[Par-*uh*-**dok**-si-kuh l Dih-**struhk**-sh*u*h n]

noun. Manipulating oneself into trading reality for a drug-laden alternative in an effort to stave off penetrating pain.

"In searching for salvation, oftentimes, the result is self-destruction."

It is at these times that my being becomes dysfunctional, and I am unable to accept life on life's terms.

At this climactic point, I am now existing in the state of an addict. I have taken on the portrayal, the abundance of destructive characteristics and the slurring lines of the addict's speech.

In my demoralizing flight of escapism, my subconscious is protesting against everything my conscious mind is performing.

I have now entered an overwhelming battle plot, a fight for unwithered pieces of sanity. My mind begins to dishevel and the veins in my heart cease to pulsate.

So what commenced as a role-playing addiction has adjourned into a disintegration or soul-saving contradiction.

D.E.N.I.A.L. [dih-**nahy**-*uh* l]
acronym. Don't Even Know I Am Lying

"*A fantastical cocktail of prescription and psychedelic drugs that places one in an altered state of being.*"

I was a learjet—it was inevitable I would crash into the airport terminal. And if I hung onto one wing, I was bound to get a discount flight to the port of Disasterville.

In this haze of my life, I could buy polar or sell polar. I had gone from my father's early death when I was seventeen to running off to a new life in

Texas, in and out of mood swings, weaving through bipolar like a reject fighter pilot.

Insightful Denial

1995

When emotional pain sets in,

It feels as though you must insidiously repent for all
your sins.

The pain penetrates you deep, like a bloody,

gouging knife. Shreds and mutilates your entire life.

You are left all alone to glue the pieces back
together.

Yet your body and mind are eerily drained.

Your existence is weak as a limp feather.

You pray that this perpetual pain will someday
subside.

But the joke's on you, buckle up for the perilous
ride.

A ride through the future, past the excuses of the
shallow,

Running from today so you can confront reality's
tomorrow.

You've lost your precious sense of self,

A commodity you'll need to regain.

Don't be ashamed—recovery's your primary task,

So reach out tighter than before and believe in your destiny to grasp.

Freedom from Bouldering Bondage

January 1995

Just say no to drugs! Drugs are the ultimate obscenity—a perversion of the innate drive to preserve one's soul from trauma.

The newest potent drug of the 90's era is what many refer to as "crack" or "rock." One would take such an awful obliteration only if there is a crack in one's soul.

A "rock" starts out as All Mighty, an illuminating force field, protecting.

Even through the destruction of my life, I never did crack (or even most drugs), but saw those around me in the slums of Houston wither in the shadow of their power.

There's an innocence lost. The newborn soul knows only safety and simple comfort. Yet as the dangers of the world crack, embitter, and age that newborn, the "rock" can become a rolling stone.

It's not a drug for the rich of soul or rich of wallet.

And when you've driven a thousand miles from New York to Texas in a $500 jalopy, from breezy to trouble as thick as the discarded bottoms of oil drums, you might need a pick-me-up.

And that's the crux of the matter—we're all just decomposing pebbles, rocks loose beneath the stone drive of someone far more powerful. And if we can unite to believe in one another and in ourselves, that newborn soul may see daylight again.

The Stillness of the Darkness

1996-1997

Why must I experience heartache, torment, and

despair?

It feels like an injustice.

A life sentence. It's just not fair—

I feel scared, battered, naked and bare.

The serpent stares me down, venomously hissing

while I am fighting and resisting.

Thankfully, the lion and the lamb lay by my side to

protect me

and save my soul. Yet, with all the

darkening anguish, will I ever

feel rejuvenated and whole?

That is undoubtedly God's greatest goal.

I have been paralyzed by depression.

It's as if it's a recession.

Turning backwards to lingering thoughts and

mistakes from yesteryear.

I will be left alone in a snake pit of rumination and

frightening fear.

How long will I ruminate, correlate, and agitate?

I know with every breath this is not my fate.

Letters

Sophia,

I haven't had a computer for a week, so I just
received your message.

I am so sorry about all this stuff with Sarai. I have
seen her several times and I can really see a
difference in her behavior since she left for Tulsa.

She fired me as a therapist (so we can spend more
friendly time together) but that just won't happen.
Sarai has lost a lot of weight, and she continues to
do so, but her mental status is about the same as
several years ago, except not so hostile and rageful.
I don't know how to help anymore. It is probably

best that you don't let her know that we discuss her
and her situation. She would rage at the both of us.

I think that Sarai will have to work out her life for
herself. She will have to find out that she needs help
before she can accept help. Let's stay in touch. I can
be the one on the other end of the email to listen if
nothing else. I know that you must feel so powerless
and helpless. I feel sad for you. It is very hard to

know that your child needs help, but you can't help.
We can pray that the situation changes.

Joanne

1997

Sophia,

I just received your letter the other day. Thank you
for thinking of me.

I have not heard from Sarai much lately either. I
can't believe that she would humble herself enough
to live in a group home.

Actually, I am glad that she has decided to do that.
Sarai is not good at setting her own rules, nor living
by anyone else's either. She must be doing better, as
she is making a good decision this time.

I am glad that she is moving back East. She has
been running for years now. It is time she went back
to deal with real life.

I also watched the events of the funeral Saturday
morning. I think that the reason Princess Diana was

so dear to everyone's hearts is because she lived visibly what many people live privately...rejection and being misunderstood. I think that we all deal with those issues daily and her life and death represent a part of each one of us. Her death really affected billions of people. I think that she personally touched more people in a short time span than any other person that has ever lived. There is more to her death than meets the eye. Rather like a Joan of Arc thing, I think that there is something universal going on here.

Joanne

Sophia,

I am glad that Sarai is returning to your wing. This will be a real test for you. I hope that you can hold up, be firm, and set firm boundaries. If you can, the

trial relationship just might work. Sarai can work
and she must. She needs to lose the last of her

Jewish American Princess mentality (which she prides herself on.)

Sarai probably shouldn't know that we communicate often. She would use it against you.

Joanne

The Final Answer

1997

Caught up in a black web of deception.

Lost sight of my true perception.

Searching for the angelic light.

Time is a relentless, paralyzing fright.

Am I worthy of God's everlasting love?

Does He hear my prayers from up above?

Will He grant me the footprints in the sand?

Will He help to keep me protected and grounded on
solid land?

Does the direction I travel lead me to the Holy
Gate?

Is all of life just lucid fate?

Will my higher power forgive me for my mistakes?

I ask for restitution for love's sake!

Will my thorn grow into a gallant rose?

Will He keep me strong through life's treacherous
lows?

Can I take his strength and conquer the Devil's

wrath?

Can I immerse myself in a sacred bath?

If all men are created equal, then why do some
souls deplete?

Why do others survive while so many give into
defeat?

Will I serve my purpose for the love of God?

Will the saints of heaven comfort me with the staff
and rod?

Can the veins in my heart continue to dance?

Can poetic justice lead to tantalizing romance?

I ponder these thoughts each day of my existence.

Have I found and accepted myself unconditionally
and without resistance?

Does my page in the book of life await me still?

Can the final answer of love guide me to the top of
the hill?

If the mind stays receptive, does the dream live on?

If the heart battles the evil trance, is life and love
ever really gone?

Sweet Land of Liberty

1997

Life is sometimes of the extreme
It's not always how it may seem
It has moments of darkness and moments
    that gleam
There are many different experiences
Some are good and some are bad
Some are of elation and some are sad
There are many lessons we learn from which
    we grow
One of life's finest is "you reap what you
    sow"
This much I know to be true
Being holy and righteous is something we
    can all do
To follow a moral quest
To derive meaning from spiritual lessons is
    the test
To acquire the Ten Commandments and
    surmise
Their contents to their fullest point and head
To be spiritually fed

So we are by Heaven led
To practice to live laugh and love
This will make the angels and God happy
     above
With all the birds flying freely in droves
Including blue jays, red cardinals, and white
     doves
To create the freedom and colors of the
     American flag
Which will never diminish or lag

Rising Glori to New Heights

Everything is good in its season
Everything has a rhyme and a reason
Some escape injustices while others end with
    treason
I have felt imprisoned and held captive
Subject to hostage by mental illness yet by the grace
    of God I have risen
Risen from the ashes of contamination,
Condemnation rumination ruination and despair
Has any of my suffering been justified or fair
There were lessons to be learned
I wanted self-evolution for this I have yearned
In order to have victory and awareness I needed
    insight
I needed to shed and rid myself of the darkness and
    enter into the light
I am triumphant
I have won
I will have more than my daily moments in the sun
Radiating and penetrating through all the universe
    as one

God's Great-full Grace

My imagination has gone wild,
Thinking back to the days when I was a
    child.
Playing, dreaming, acting, living to be free.
Realizing I am unique; there is only one me.
The journey of a thousand miles begins with
the first step, the first stride.
Lord, keep me well and present so I don't
    hide—hide from all others,
including my Christian sisters and brothers,
Scared to interact.
What a sad and lonely fact.
I have flatlined into mental arrest.
However will I again be my baseline or
    best?
I feel disconnected from everyone and
    everything.
I have no desire to create, express, worship,
    or sing.
I desperately need an angel's prayer and
    wing.

How long will this vegetative, dark state of
     mind exist?

The demons I must resist!

Upon justice and cleansing, I insist.

The phoenix rises from the ashes; I must do
     the same.

I will prove to them all that I am fully sane.

1993-1997 J. Belle (Joanne)

2004-2011 YoungBlood

2012-2014 Tania

Utopia 33 Euphoria

Dedicated to three angelic healers

I

I have arrived, survived the diagnosis

And the poor prognosis of my mental dis-ease.

Texas, Texas—the unexpected nexus of my despair.

Before I got there, I theorized the Lone Star State

As a breath of fresh air,

And in that great big state, an angel was waiting

there.

J. Belle, Joanne, my therapist, my friend, when the

Confusion was too much;

When tides of bipolar terror came in under the

Pale moonlight of self-distrust—

When I could not be kind to myself or those I met.

But with her sense of benevolence, I could forget

The errors of my single-sided arrogance.

"You reap what you sow," she said.

And she sewed this in me in every session, in every

    action,

Until I was able to do unto others what others

    would...

And New York, it came calling back.

The life of an advertising exec, account manager

To be exact. All that pressure,

That night cry for solace, that's when Youngblood,

My therapist here, in the business of her proud

vibrancy

Would with me connect.

Yet, I was faced the problems of progress

From her, the answers I would implore.

"Youngblood, oh how wrong it is to be grouped

here in this place with these sick people."

"But Lori, you are not better or worse. Only concern

Yourself with change.

With overcoming your sense of entitlement. And

then from This world or any other you

Won't be estranged."

I worked with her for seven years. We sandblasted

my darkest,

Deepest fears: honest and sincere.

There were so many issues.

There weren't enough bulk-volume Kleenex tissues.

A recurring theme, that river of judgment from me

did stream.

My childhood brought me sense of entitlement

And, with this healer, we toned it down as a team.

Tanya, loving and nurturing; she was my greatest

fan.

Even through my eight hospitalizations in a two

year span.

While under her care, life was less than fair!

I had eight hospitalizations in a two year span.

I was like saturated worms suffocating in a can.

At the time, I was receiving shock treatment on a

regular basis.

Before the shock treatment, I had oceans and oceans

Of emotions—so I kept asking her,

"Why can't I cry? Did my spiritual insides die?

Why can't I feel true happiness and belly laugh like

the Good-ol' days?"

I constantly pray this was just a temporary phase.

What happened to all my creativity? Sensitivity?

Then the psychosis rocked my sanity and I

attempted Suicide for the second time.

And there she was, to cut through my black and

white TV thinking.

To comfort me in the ICU when I was still reeling,

to use twenty years of experience

In calming my errant ways of sinking.

I attempted to master

My mind over pain

To quell the kuelling, kvetching voice

Driving me insane.

Driving me, driving me, driving me

To try and end my life again.

Would this fatalistic behavior end?

When? Oh, when?

She taught me to remain humble and

Not be so grandiose. To have patience

With the other patients

That each individual has worth.

She stated to me, "everyone has a varying level of

mental illness.

Some of the people won't change, grow, or get

well."

But the way I put it—they stay stuck in stillness,

unchanging hell!"

Many months after I had this suicide attempt,

Tanya questioned if she was such a wonderful

therapist,

Why couldn't she preempt?

I explained that I was so out of touch with reality.

If I dared share my thoughts,

I'd be locked away for good. I was so afraid.

I don't think anyone could have understood.

Traveling so many miles, traversing so many trials,

there is a sense of transition from this beating center

of a once-paused heart.

I have arrived.

I have survived this insidious, peculiar ride.

I am fully aware, mindful, and alive.

A new chapter, a new book.

A completely and utterly astounding,

Resounding, rebounding outlook.

The lessons these living angels taught me

Are the verses and these flawed flows are my

catchy hook.

Conclusions of
Grandeur

Why do you Look Familiar?
Do I Know You?

It was an epic of sorts. They came to Ellis Island in droves and many changed their names in hopes of also changing their lives. It was like a long-standing poker game and the voyagers prayed that not only would they be playing with a full deck, but that they would ascertain a Royal Flush in their new land of America. The only problem being that many new Americans were dealt the joker and its jester cap lingered over the dynamics of dysfunction and despair. My paternal ancestors fled from the fires of the Russian pogroms. My maternal ancestors fled from the poverty and lack of education in Hungary. My family would settle in Brooklyn, New York with many new hopes, aspirations, and ideas. Both my maternal and paternal grandparents would marry while they were teenagers. They were still mere children themselves taking on the great responsibility of raising their own families.

How could this concept ever work? My mother was one of three children. My father was one of five. At times, all of them were like starving actors in a quest for notoriety and an Oscar. They were playing different roles at different times. Sometimes, they were understudies rehearsing their lines; not quite sure of the words' accuracy and not quite sure if they would ever be heard.

At other times, they encapsulated the roles of the scapegoat, the black sheep, the caretaker, the good or bad child, the martyr, the hero, and so much more. For the most part, they were just children trying to seek the approval of their parents and grandparents. They were trying to make everyone happy. Would that failed, unrealistic goal leave them feeling safe enough to grow into functioning and independent adults? Did it leave them with the proper tools to parent properly?

My parents met as high school sweethearts and joined the sacred union and foundation of marriage at twenty one years of age. As a family, they survived death, infidelity, abuse, divorce, addictions, tragedy, and many of life's other losses. Yet through all the thick and the thin they remained intact as a family.

I remember my childhood so vividly. For the most part, it was a colorful array of rainbows, shooting stars and crescent moons. Unfortunately, at times least expected, the darkness permeated. My parents settled on suburban Long Island and I would be granted, by God, one older sibling. My brother was a tough act to follow. He was smart, handsome, resilient, charming and so very talented. In the midst of the dark days, he was angry, jealous, and unsure of his brilliant capabilities. He was my father's little protégé and he taught him golf, poker, and other sports. My father also taught him about the business world. More importantly, he taught him what it meant to be an honorable man and to fight for the survival of a loving marriage during those times when it was failing miserably. My brother was my mother's prince; the first born, the only son.

My father was a beautiful soul; charismatic, loving, witty, and wise. He spent his days building those people up that couldn't find their own inner strength. Though he was a high school dropout, he was street smart; not only able to adapt to all kinds of people but to all kinds of situations as well.

My mother was simply magnificent inside and out. Her outer beauty resembled that of Sophia Lauren and Jackie Onassis while her inner beauty paralleled Florence Nightingale. She was a caretaker; compassionate, kind, vibrant, and strong willed. My mother was a dedicated daughter, wife, and mother. She was primarily a housewife. She spent much of her time raising my brother and me while my father was away on business trips attempting to build an empire that would provide his family with the finer things in life. My mother had a great love of animals, especially horses. She was an equestrian and would do shows throughout Long Island. I particularly enjoyed the elite of the

Hampton Classic. This became her daily therapy session—her Xanax. Then I came along. And I asked everything of life and would stop at nothing to retrieve it. I was the only granddaughter on my mother's side for a long time. I was doted over; smothered with love and attention. I was the only daughter and, undoubtedly, the fairy princess with the ethereal wand. My mother kept me looking meticulous. She treated me like a china doll. I was her prized trophy. I was her chance to exist all over again and to somehow rectify the mistakes of her own scorned childhood. Many times, her expectations of me were too great; as if I was a gymnast or a pole vaulter. I certainly was Daddy's little girl. Much of the time, we had an undying and unspoken kismet bond. Wherever he took my brother, I was just a few steps behind. We would travel together to his antique business, serenading one another with songs of our inspirations Frank Sinatra and Barbara Streisand in his newly-polished Cadillac. He was my great professor and profoundly taught me the indispensable lessons of life and all the love it had to offer.

My maternal grandfather and paternal grandmother would send for me in the summertime. I spent my days on Collins Avenue in Miami Beach, Florida and on Hallandale Beach Boulevard in Fort Lauderdale, Florida. My mother's father was more like a father to me than to his own children. I looked to him for reassurance and recognition. He would take me to all the cabaret shows, on cruises, and to the "Early Bird Special."

My father's mother was a dynamic force. After losing her husband, she became a very independent woman. She was funny, classy, courageous, and lovely. I adored being with her. Everywhere we went, from the supermarket, to the bank, to the cleaners, people would respectfully refer to her as Ms. Tatarsky and graciously smile at her when she entered a room. I felt beyond special when I was with her and I was her little Pally. She was also obsessed with superficial looks and perfection. It became apparent as I grew older that my nose and body image were not to her liking. They were too large according to her standards. I felt the only way I could survive her condemnation was if I was a famous wax sculpture at Madame Tussaud's Museum or if I was a finely painted masterpiece by Botticelli or Erté. I felt as if this glorious rose garden of generosity, empathy, and uniqueness that was being cultivated inside my soul was suppressed by her harsh judgments.

My mother's mother was an incredible woman. When her husband left her for another woman, she single handedly raised a family and worked long, hard hours to survive. I called her my Bubalah. She was so much fun to be around. She cooked for my family when we were sick and always had a batch of "Jewish penicillin," chicken soup, on call for us. She took me clothes shopping at Bloomies and accompanied my brother and me to many Broadway shows. My Bubalah was awesome and was my greatest gift of all my unwrappings.

When life became difficult, tumultuous, and dreary and I could no longer seek comfort in my blood family, I looked elsewhere. I realized there were many venues where family existed. I found the sisters and brothers I never had in endearing friends and grandparents. I found mother and father figures in teachers, therapists, and older spirits. Ultimately, I came to the revelation that we are all heirs and heiresses of God's Royal Kingdom. We are truly never without family. We are never truly alone.

Peter 2:9 "But you are the chosen people, a royal priesthood, a holy nation, a people belonging to God, that you may declare the praises of Him who called you out of the darkness into His wonderful light. Once, you were not a people but now you are a people of God; once you had not received mercy but now you have received mercy."

Psalm 5: 11 But let all those that put their trust in thee rejoice: let them ever shout for joy because thou defendest them: let them also that love thy

name be joyful in thee.

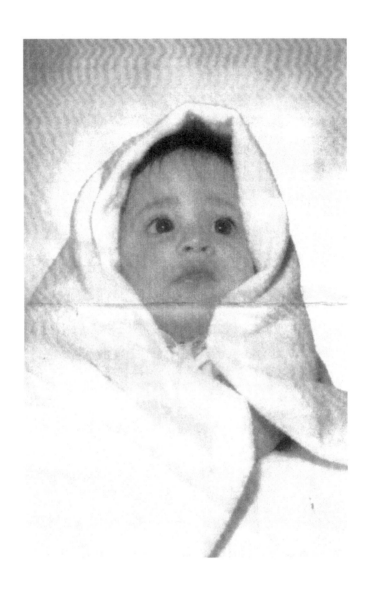

Diet has Die in It/
Healthy has Heal in It

I'll never forget sneaking down the hallway in the middle of the night like a scavenger scouring the cabinets and refrigerator. I was always searching for the next bite to fill the pit of insecurity in me. Wandering in the dark, hiding, waiting for a mason to patch up the infrastructure of uncertainty. It was pretty simple: competition. Yes, it's good until it becomes the only thing one breathes. In my upper middle-class childhood, there was always competition—scrutiny—to come out on top in beauty, grades, wit, personality. All calculated atop some New York iceberg of child show and tell, shining bright as the Empire State Building at night. I refused to go to sleep-away camp at age eleven for fear of being made fun of by the other girls when I would undress. (In my distorted imagination, I blew up my weight of 130 lbs into a communal game of hungry-hungry hippos.) My eating addiction progressed. My attempts to solve the image equation were many: starvation, the Cabbage Soup Diet, the Atkins Diet, the Scarsdale Diet, the Ice Cream Diet, Weight Watchers, The Diet Center, NutriSystem, Jenny Craig, and excessive exercise. Results eluded me; I was powerless over this insurmountable addiction. By the time I was twenty one I had ballooned from one hundred thirty pounds to two hundred fifty pounds due to deepening depression and the tremendous amounts of psychotropic drugs I was given. I was unrecognizable. My body was like a racetrack of stretch marks. The shame I felt was enormous.

My soul was beaten. The disease was closing in on me. I was gasping for oxygen and crying for relief.

Guess I wasn't such a shrewd businesswoman after all. I dabbled in bulimia to lighten up and would dine at the finest restaurants, only to glide home and regurgitate for fear of (once again) the number on the scale. The weight on my shoulders! I distanced myself from my friends and became isolated like a caged animal. God forbid anyone knew my secret. I was obese and utterly miserable. By the time I reached my thirties, my weight had escalated to three hundred pounds. I had severe insulin-dependent diabetes and sleep apnea; I was desperate, sweating profusely, and couldn't breathe. As the breath of life was slowly leaving me, all I could think of was how society places these false images through our impressionable heads that we're to appear as Greek gods and goddesses, sculpted like a Rodan. Never taking into account how anything less might drive us to consume more and more.

I made a decision to undergo gastric bypass surgery. I ignored the risks, for I had already felt that enemy (food) ridicule me hourly. I recovered from my surgery and the weight started to dissipate. It was always about the number on the scale; if it was a small number, it was akin to winning the lotto, while a heavy number meant the mark of the beast. I went from three hundred pounds to one hundred eighty pounds. Life was renewed and my health problems vanished. Yet the demons still crept up on me. I could no longer binge to take away the disappointments and anguish of everyday life. I lost my sacred friend—food. I faced my denial and realized, surgery or not, I was a hardcore food addict. I joined Overeaters Anonymous and conceded that I was powerless over this monstrosity. So I came to realize that a power greater than myself could restore me to sanity. I couldn't comprehend what sanity meant. I had always been so erratic and irrational when it came to food, body image, and weight. I attended Twelve Step meetings and met fellow sufferers. There were people of all sizes, backgrounds, and colors. We were all faced with the enemy; the stranger that grabs onto its victims. We made peace with food addiction by facing it and gaining accountability for our food choices. We shifted to build a healthy relationship with food as we would a new friend or loved one. We knew this process would take time, but would reward us with freedom instead of being trapped by nervous whims.

I read stories from the <u>Twelve Step Big Book</u> and could relate to each one. I obtained a sponsor and committed my food to her. Diet has die in it; healthy has heal in it. If one lives and dies by specific diets, they miss where the diet comes from. Diet is no substitution for learning what will bring you encompassing wellness. But health is a part of the spirit and of physical constitution Yet will the addict ever feel like they're not locked up in their habits?

To many, all of these tools were a recipe for success. However, I couldn't relinquish my friend. We could not part ways. I didn't know how to control the emotional turmoil in my world. Food was my interception pass. Food was my glorious touchdown. So, was I to always cultivate this unhealthy marriage with food addiction? Was I to go to my resting place a full-fledged food addict? I aspired to the aura of Princess Diana: of being beloved, kind, and noble. She was the Princess of

Wales and I would not concede to being the biggest of whales. I would continually work on emulating a beautiful spirit within, knowing eventually I would feel beautiful outwardly. Just food for thought?

Romans 8:28 And we know all things work together for good to them that love God; to them who are the called according to his purpose.

The Garden of Eating

I explored my spirituality and theological beliefs. To be a Jew, or not to be, was my question. If Jesus was a Jewish lawyer or doctor as opposed to a carpenter, would all the Jews be more receptive to His message? I studied the Bible. It was puzzling to me and I wondered if, when they wrote it, they were drinking too much wine at the last supper. Too much sipsy sipsy. Were they tipsy tipsy? I pondered so much. I wondered if Adam and Eve had been in the Garden of Eating instead of Eden. It would have been plentiful and they would never have been tempted by the poisonous apple. When I chose to be a Messianic Jew, many didn't understand and thought I was a mess of a Jew. But to me, it was the best of both worlds. I could honor Yeshua as my Lord and Savior, yet I could ingest the culture, traditions, and foods of Judaism. Part of the reason I would embrace both was because in Christianity they focus on the Ten Commandments. Whereas, in order to receive blessings in Judaism, there are six hundred thirteen commandment commentaries of Rabbi Simlai to abide by. In essence, it was easier to abide by the ten. Thank God, it was only a fable that becoming a Messianic Jew would force me to give up bagels with a schmear of cream cheese, whitefish, lox, or sable. Always tasted heavenly at the Sunday morning breakfast table. Jewish penicillin, aka Matzo ball chicken soup, my chance to get better and regroup. A gnash of a knish was always delish. I could honor Yom Kippur or eat yummy kipper. I never understood why they only gave the Jews one day to atone for their sins when in fact the Catholics could repeatedly sin and, as long as they went to confession, those sins would be absolved. Provided I didn't let Passover pass over, I could enjoy the seder, and, of course, I would rush-a-home-a for Rosh Hashanah. On Chanukah, I would be in the presence of so many great family members and friends and receive so many awesome presents. The greatest thing was Christmas was just around the corner and the same would be applicable. So ultimately, being a believer and a Jew for Jesus wasn't a loss of Judaism, but a gain of Christianity. And the best part was, I could indeed keep my Jewish chutzpah—which in layman's terms meant I had more balls than a Christmas tree.

Psalm 23:6 Goodness and mercy shall follow me all the days of my life.

Could It Be Satan?

The light and the darkness don't always blend well together. It was April 17th, 2007. We were close to the Easter holiday and this was the day that I would make the acquaintance of the maimed, the ordained, and the insane. My life would be altered forever and I would learn what it meant to live with a life-long physical disability. I remember the events of that wretched day vividly. I had been ambushed by the dragon of depression again. I was presently unemployed; let go from my last position because of the troubling economy. I thought about the last *ten* years of my career in the advertising and marketing arena. I missed the drive I once had to excel and reach the pinnacle of the sales force. I missed all the interaction I had with all the different business owners. I felt misguided, as if the fire in my belly had been stomped out. My days were empty and my talents were no longer recognized. I was like an injured racehorse at the Kentucky Derby. The finish line was nowhere in sight. I chuckled when I thought about the highs and the lows of my lengthy career. I remembered the ambitious days of pounding the pavement, not coming back to the office without a sale. The pressure was stifling; yet the adrenaline rush was like a tiebreaker in a Subway Series.

I sat in dismay when I rehashed the days when I took advantage of the freedom of my outside sales position. I was like a martial arts master, trying to remain disciplined; falling short to the commands. Some days, it was nothing more than French Manicures, tanning salons, Starbucks, escargot, surf and turf, and beef Carpaccio—even a wild menage a trois on one occasion. I manipulated the system and justified it in my torrid mind. I thought about how many more times I had done so in other arenas of my life. What rang true was how often I had manipulated the system of spirituality. At times, I was so righteous and willing to speak my truth for the benevolence of the Lord. Other times, I held hands with the sinful sorcerer and skipped through the avenue of catastrophes blindly, yet willingly. The depression I was experiencing was more severe than I had ever succumbed to before. I couldn't relate to life around me and felt dead within. I would sit in the park surrounded by the exquisite cherry blossoms and they would appear to be nothing more than wilted weeds. I would witness a beautiful child flying a kite and feel numb. I would glare at the glistening water and wish that I could drown in its miraculous formation. I would spend time with friends and family and it was if they were strangers that I had never even met.

I was experiencing complete and utter anhedonia: lack of pleasure in everything and anything. I hardly slept while I was depressed. I worried incessantly about my futile future and punished myself for the mistakes of my sinful past. I desperately desired sleep just to flee the disturbing racket in my mind. It was like a non stop, 24/7 heavy metal concert playing over and over again. I wanted to be clear and awake to a new reality, a day shy of the multitude of heartbreaks. I ingested an overdose of psychotropic drugs and passed out on my floor. When I awoke seven hours later, I was disoriented and my left leg was as inflamed as a tree trunk. I couldn't walk and I was trapped, all alone, in my apartment with no use of a telephone. I literally crawled out of my apartment and screamed for help. My neighbors, who were former nuns, found me and called 911. I lay in the hospital, in agony, while the doctors misdiagnosed my condition and kept me waiting for eleven long, surreal hours to perform emergency surgery for what they realized was a rare condition called Compartment Syndrome. I was left with permanent nerve damage to my left foot and a more than noticeable limp. Was it to be the agony of the de-feet? Would I rise and walk firmly to the occasion and conquer my disability? Or would I fall prey to the injustices and self pity of much of the human race? If those with prosthetic legs could run marathons, why couldn't I even muster up enough energy or strength to walk from the bedroom to the refrigerator and back again?

I may not be a doctor or have a stream of letters of my name. In reality, due to the severe symptoms of my mental illness, I wasn't even able to complete college. Yet throughout my many travels and life experiences, I have not only been through countless times when I was given the third degree by many negative people I had allowed to enter my mind's world, but have also gained an enormous amount of awareness, wisdom, and insight. If only the doctors had conferred with me, I might have been spared a permanent physical limitation. It was my assessment that Compartment Syndrome was when women don't have enough compartments in their purses, pocketbooks, or bags to lug all of their makeup and other goodies around. Case closed. I was also given an emergency surgery called a facetectomy, which could have meant I had an excellent sense of fashion, but was actually meant to remove a painfully damaged impacted facet of my spine. The saddest part was that, after my suicide attempt, I became a bag lady; a vagabond after I lost my studio apartment of nine years. My gracious mother not only took me into her one-bedroom apartment but, at age sixty five, single handedly cleared out my entire apartment while I lay immobilized in bed in a depressive stupor. I was feeling worthless, filled with racing and disorganized thoughts and fearing the uncertainty of my future—lost in this land of Oz. yet without the lion's courage and no Yellow Brick Road to follow. Over the next two years, my relationship with my mother, and my life in general, were challenging— to say the least. So many days, I would just lay in bed and ruminate on overwhelming, negative thoughts. I'd smoke cigarette after cigarette to pass the time. I had no structure or job. Each moment felt like it was endless. I couldn't even perform simple tasks such as food shopping, laundry, or cooking for myself. However, even when I was as healthy as a horse in the stable, these mundane tasks never called to me. I always tried to brush them off on someone else. I had what is called Executive Malfunction; which basically meant I could accomplish large tasks, yet the simple ones would stump me.

It was as though my mom was taken hostage on this disheartening journey with me. When I was depressed, she was depressed. She would always say:

"Lori, when you are happy, I will be happy."

That is how much she loved me and wanted me to recover from the terrors of mental illness. While living with her, I was seeing a top psychiatrist. He would constantly try new combinations of drugs on me. Yet nothing would sustain my wellness. He suggested ECT, shock treatment, to stop the depression and psychosis I was still experiencing. The psychosis was terrorizing. Now, instead of believing I was the devil, responsible for all evil on the earth, I believed I was being chased by good old Lucifer. One incident, I recall, was being so scared of Satan that I took pretzel logs and made crosses all over my bed for protection. I prayed to the Lord to help me.

So it was back to square one at the hospital. And now, instead of shock treatment once a month, I received bonuses three times a week. I always woke up from anesthesia weak, with a headache, unable to clearly think. It took about a day to recuperate. I grew to hate this treatment and to believe it barbaric.

What do you do when the last resort doesn't work? Do you just settle for being out of control and berserk? For the most part, I was compliant, occasionally defiant, which made my mental illness non-reliant. No matter what, the medicines wouldn't sustain my condition. It was constant hospital readmission. I fought so hard for my stability, reliability; the probability of living my life to the fullest with passion, fashion, and grace. I was to come face to face with my Creator. There was no greater Director or Moderator.

Psalm 4:8 I will both lay me down in peace and sleep, for thou, Lord, only makest me dwell in safety.

Jailhouse Shock

The year was 1997 and the world had lost its Princess Diana. I, too, lost the sparkle and fairy dust in my princess wand. This would be the year that the Grim Reaper would meet me in combat. He would not only attempt to take my life once, but he would attempt his pathetic ploys twice. Things were going relatively well for the moment and then circumstances drastically shifted. I was working long hours for a large healthcare company as an independent sales representative and doing tremendous amounts of traveling. I had many friends as colleagues and my mind was constantly stimulated. It was the day before Thanksgiving and there were hurricane conditions in Houston.

I needed to deliver products to a client's home. So I ventured onto Interstate 10. I drove cautiously in the torrential downpour and, within seconds, a vehicle cut me off. I jammed on my brakes only to hydroplane four lanes into the medium. Suddenly, a Greyhound bus smashed into me, leaving my car resembling an archaic accordion. I could feel my father's presence from the other side. I could imagine turning the key to the Gates of Heaven. Yet I wasn't ready to relinquish all my uncrossed dreams.

The jaws of life appeared and cut me out of what was left of my vehicle. I was in so much pain, I practically lay there unconscious. I broke my back in three spots and was placed in a back brace. The treating doctors were amazed that I wasn't left permanently paralyzed from the neck down. Though the grace of God went I. In due time, I miraculously healed and returned to work. I continued to travel and attended a conference in Memphis, Tennessee. The magic and the mania had returned. Suddenly, without knowing why, I was screaming so loudly at the conference that security had to restrain and remove me. In the process, I lost my pocket book which contained all the accessible cash I had to my name. I literally panhandled my way back to Texas. I drove erratically while the radio in my car was reciting and commanding messages to me. I was undoubtedly back in the pits of Hell's hallucinations.

I had plans to meet friends at the Five Star Crescent Hotel in Dallas. I arrived early and entertained myself by roaming the lobby. It was a glorious sight of breathtaking flower arrangements, marble floors, and signed art works. I was there for hours, asking all kinds of outlandish questions of the staff. My friends never showed up. The clock struck midnight and I was arrested. It was at this same hotel where, months prior, I had driven up in my friend's brand new Porsche Carrerra and ate pâté de foie gras at the hotel's acclaimed restaurant. I smoked Macanudo cigarillos at the bar and sipped aged Cognac. Now I was nothing more than an abused animal left out in the frigid cold with a leash tied around my neck.

What happened next was deplorable. It was as if the dark side had ransacked my body. It's so ironic how life can change on a dime. One minute, I was on top of the world. Now all I could do was wish to escape the brutality of it. I was charged with criminal trespassing. I was placed in a holding cell. I started to recite:

"For I know the plans I have for you, declares the Lord: plans to prosper you and not harm you; plans to give you hope and a future. Then you will call on me and come and pray to me and I will listen to you. You will seek me and find me when you seek me with all your heart. I will be found by you, declares the Lord, and will bring you back from captivity." (Jeremiah 29:11-14.)

I prayed that all of us locked up here would make it out alive. My thoughts were racing faster than the Orient Express. I was really sick and begged the police to give me medication. They kept laughing; commenting that I wasn't "crazy" and didn't need medication. I spent four days in a jail cell having audible and visual hallucinations. My meals consisted of bologna and cheese sandwiches. This was a far cry from the Beluga Caviar I had tasted as a youngster.

When I was finally released, I felt as if I had just emerged from a pile of rubble. Would I ever be the same again? My essence was wholly impeded. The doves that used to encircle my spirit now lay bloodstained and dormant.

I returned to Houston scarred spiritually and mentally. I felt like a knocked out prize fighter who had just gone twelve rounds with Jesus and the Devil. I was hospitalized in what was beginning to feel like my yearly timeshare. I would hysterically cry for days on end. I had to give up my apartment and temporarily reside in a group home. It was as if I were back in the holding cell. But now, instead of being surrounded by people who committed crimes, I was in the company of schizophrenics and wayward, drug-addled young people. That's where my journey of roughly five years ended. I was deep in my broken heart of Texas. I would finally lift my head from the sand and reunite with my mother in New York.

Would I ever truly break free from the bars that barricaded my soul or would I remain a criminal trespasser on my continuing path of purity and peaceful progression?

Deuteronomy 31:6 Where God told His people, "never will I foresake you.

Hebrew 4:15 In the darkest moments of life, the assurance of His loving presence gives us confidence that we are not alone. He gives us the grace to endure, the wisdom to know He is working and the assurance that Christ can empathize with our weaknesses.

Deep in my Heart of Texas

Hefty garbage bags and a $500 car with doors strapped on by string. These carried my clothes, my shame, and my hopes of escape from New York to Houston. And Houston, we did have a problem. I had gone up to two hundred fifty pounds from the meds prescribed to me. I had gone down the path of guilt and depression over even possessing my mental illness. No one, apart from my mother, had any idea I had left. I was on a quest to recapture the pure heart of a child. On my journey, I slept in many motels and would confiscate the Gideon Bibles. Nothing to be giddy about at this point. I was aching to feel part of God's universe again. I had lost my faith from all the heartache and trauma. When I was a little girl, I would pray every night that the Creator would keep my friends and family happy, healthy, and safe. I was like a magician, continually pulling the rabbit from the hat. For so very long my prayers were answered.

But then the Serpent reared its ugly head and hissed at my existence. Pandemonium broke loose and I was like a fugitive on the run looking for shelter. Many days later, I arrived at the White Deer Run Treatment Center for Dual Diagnosis of Mental Illness and Addictions. The metamorphosis would begin. Not only would I stare Lucifer in the eye, demanding, "no more," but I would have the great pleasure of meeting the mesmerizing eyes of the Savior.

It was in treatment that I learned about compassion for others suffering from mental challenges. It was in treatment that I realized how living with addictions was a stranglehold. I realized how it gripped and suffocated your every breath. I came to terms with setting boundaries between myself and others. I had so much rage inside of me that I was like an erupting volcano spewing lava. I began to face my fears; some evident, some hidden. It was then that I would fear; either face everything and recover or forget everything and run. It was then that I would introduce myself to the grave denial that I was presently living. Slowly, my soul was withering away. I stayed in treatment for months.

I began to heal and know that the sun would rise as I would. Each day was a new gift to be unwrapped—to rejoice in its splendor. One of the greatest gifts I was given was the friendship and mentoring of the center's head therapist, Joanne. She was one of the most ravishing, kind, and enlightened human beings I had ever encountered. Now that the student was ready, the teacher would appear. She would not only become my long term therapist, but act as my surrogate mother. She stepped in where there was a huge void. After treatment, I decided to remain in Houston.

Financially, I was granted child survivor claim disability and that was exactly the role that I would portray. As long as I had a breath, I would fight to be a child survivor.

The only apartment I could afford was in a very dangerous part of town. Primarily, I slept on the floor, as I couldn't afford to buy furniture. Sucked into the environment around me, and with self-esteem in short supply, I would give my body up to all sorts of lowlifes because I thought I deserved it. I had been used to Ralph Lauren clean-cut prototypes but I was horrible to myself.

Yet I did manage to eat at all the top-rated soup kitchens, "restaurants", and valet park my five hundred dollar vehicle amongst the European cars on show. I dressed in fine suits, silk blouses and scarves and vintage hats due to credit card debt and bankruptcy. I attended therapy three times a week while Joanne kept reciting to me:

"You reap what you sow."

So, deep in my heart of Texas, would my heart be resurrected or would I ultimately fall prey to spiritual cardiac arrest?

Peter 5:10: And the God of all grace, who called you to do His eternal glory in Christ, after you have suffered a little while, will Himself restore you and make you strong, firm, and steadfast.

Oy Vey

My birthday was premature. I arrived two and a half months early as my mother hemorrhaged towards death. She was left with a huge scar on her abdomen. At times, she claims I have scarred her for life. The relationship has been one of both great elation and debilitation. She treasured my every moment and I was taken care of like royalty. I was dressed like a fashion icon and fed the highest quality Gerber's. I was nurtured, held, touched, and—above all—loved.

I was taught indispensable lessons, from tying my shoes to tying up loose ends; from relating to other humans to learning the importance of sacrifice and giving. Although I was raised with money, she also gave me values and deference.

I was enamored with who my mother was. She put so much time and effort into raising me, it's as if she sublimated her own identity. She no longer just existed for herself but her every fiber went into shaping and forming me. When she was cradling me, I felt as if the world was completely at my doorstep. I could attain anything. I would run to her in the middle of the night and my nightmares would subside. She would combat the boogeyman.

So, there I was. Ultimately, I would honor my mother and father. Or would I?

The years went on and our relationship began to crumble. I started to perceive the world through my own eyes. It became transparent that what I wanted was to learn from this journey. I seemed opinionated and defiant as my ideas surfaced. I was growing into the woman that God intended me to be. Her behavior towards me bordered on abusive. She shot arrows at my self esteem. She would insult my notions and my ideas. Here I was, trying hard to become an entity that she could be proud of and she could only reject me. I had spent a lifetime trying to please this woman who had given me breath; who showed me light. Yet, at what cost? The price was my jubilation and God's dreams for me. The phenomenon was that I spent a lifetime modifying my behavior to affect my aura. To my great surprise, I woke up one day and realized that, while attempting to become the woman God wanted me to be, I was awakened to the realization that I had a lot of my mother's traits.

With that catharsis, I felt honored to have all her good traits in me. All her flaws suddenly didn't matter. I could accept her unconditionally. Once those feelings flowed, I could accept myself unconditionally. I could use the two sided mirror to see more clearly. Although at times, my mother and I were distant from each other. There would always be a special place in our hearts for one another. Our souls were entwined with mutual love, respect, and—for the most part—kindness that even a hurricane couldn't tear down. If I would have had the foresight to know I would be plagued by a chronic mental illness that would bring me into calamities, catastrophes, suicidal ideation and attempts, bankruptcies, torn relationships, arrests, arduous depressions, lack of job stability, loss of the ability to take care of myself, reckless behavior and so forth, I would have appreciated her more.

Through it all, my mom never abandoned me. She believed, even when I lay in a coma in the Intensive Care Unit, that as long as I had breath she would assure me anything was possible. I was so blessed to have her. Many families throw mentally ill loved ones to the curbside, disowning them because they are too much of a burden.

For the most part, my mother would visit me in every hospitalization. When they unlocked the doors, I would cry as if I was a small child going on the school bus for the first time without her strength, love, and protection. The indifference I once felt towards this incredible example of a woman arose from her need to control me. At times, my mother was much more quiet and reserved. I think she was bothered and concerned by my ability to open up to anyone; the fact that I was so trusting and loving. In many ways, that was a part of my personality that reminded her of my father. I believe that brought back so much of the pain of tragically and unfairly losing him. When my mom realized I was speaking my truth about my mental illness and about how being a Messianic Jew saved my life while promoting this book, she couldn't accept my honesty. So she chose to un-friend me on Facebook.

Psalm 8:3 When I consider thy heavens, the work of thy fingers, the moon and the stars which God has ordained

John 4:16: God is love
And all that dwelleth in love
Dwelleth in God

Isaiah 66:13 As a mother comforts her child, so will I comfort you and you will be comforted over Jerusalem.

Beloved

2010

The year was 1982: my father's fortieth year on this planet. He was practically one of the Rat Pack. He enjoyed Sinatra, fine food, good liquor, fast cars, beautiful women, and smoking. Inevitably, he sustained a massive heart attack leading to quadruple bypass surgery. My father endured a blood transfusion that became the beginning of the end.

Six years later, my father, due to the blood transfusion, was diagnosed with AIDS. It took him quickly and furiously a year later. The man who raised me was vital, suntanned; a fine dresser who took great care in his presentation and reputation. Monogrammed shirts, Stetson cowboy hats for those casual days. Designer suits, Cadillacs, and that refined confidence of a robust man in his prime. All of it faded into so much pain.

Panic ran through my mind as I watched him suffer. What if my mother contracted the disease from their intimate contact? What if I was left an orphan?

I wanted to cradle my father like a baby; to soothe him. I wanted to feed him and help him put more weight back on. All I could do was to unhinge my emotions and look for a fire escape from the oncoming conflagration. I didn't know how to let him go. He was my oft-sung hero! Since I was a little girl, I had idealized him. We were in sync with each others' spirits and love of life; a mere wink between daughter and dad would capture all the details of a moment.

The candles on my seventeenth birthday cake blew out and I wouldn't say a word of my wish lest it not come true. I did not want him to suffer anymore. And it was that day my heavenly father on this earthly plane would join the Father in Heaven.

It's so ironic that I was the last person to speak to my father. He uttered, with a weak and trembling breath,

"Princess, when I get out of here I'll buy you whatever you want for your birthday."

All I ever wanted was to have my family back. All I ever wanted was to feel whole again. It was as if my heart had done a pirouette and fallen. As much as I loved my father, I was enraged and felt abandoned by his demise. I wondered if I would be able to sustain a longstanding relationship ever again. I began to detach from my family and my close friends. I gave the enemy exactly what they wanted; to isolate me from any kind of comfort, strength, or support.

Would I ever be able to love completely and wholeheartedly again? Or would the fear and pain of abandonment stifle my every relationship?

2016

Looking back, I was blessed to have him even for a short while. Blessed to carry him with me even when the trauma of his death marked the beginning of my struggle with mental dis-ease. There was so much love flowing through my veins from the perpetuating Blood of Jesus. I was given an inheritance from the Almighty Kingdom; accompanied by nurturing, attention, and encouragement from teachers, coaches, friends, and family. My heart would vibrantly beat faster than a marching band. The enormous confidence I felt flowed like a waterfall leading into a warm lavender and coconut scented Jacuzzi with multi-colored koi fish.

The lessons I learned as a youngster were taught by the most compassionate and scholarly souls. They were indispensable—at times so fascinating. They were indescribable. At bedtime, I would lay my tired keppe on the soft pillow and God would hold me. Even in this upside down cake of a world which lacks much more than icing and sprinkles, I would truly never be lost even when the darkness suffocated my spirit. There was no trauma, no physical disability, no mental disorder with countless shock treatments in conjunction with memory loss that could ambush or rob me of these heavenly memories. These were sacred, savored moments handpicked just for my life's story from the Sovereign Savior. With God's help and guidance, I could hold steadfast to all my childhood mitzvahs that I could store on some flash drive and the illustrations would be as vivid and colorful as an artist's abstracts.

I had the premonition or déjà vu of Omnia Vincit Amoré ("Love Conquers All"). This infinite love that had no limits, no boundaries, would carry me through the perilous battles of my soul. I would remain victorious, sprinting alongside my Beloved Lord Emmanuel; flying high like Wonder Woman. I would be joined by the other masses of superheroes and they would all have their protective trinity shields and capes. Supernatural powers of healing miracles, for self and others, would be evident.

The animals of the carnal flesh would graciously move aside and allow all of God's animals to bring joy and unconditional love to their owners. We would finally understand what they were saying to us. There would be glittering, shimmering diamonds that ignited from each of our childlike spirits and the world would simultaneously shine brighter than ever before and the Creator would ultimately and eternally be providing the spotlight.

Isaiah 61:3 To appoint unto them that mourn in Zion, to give unto them beauty for ashes, the oil of joy for mourning, the garment of praise for the spirit of heaviness, that they might be called trees of righteousness, the planting of the Lord, that He might be glorified.

Intrinsic Fate

2001

Today in this universe
I have felt enlightenment
I was given insight
I have faced some of my fears
I have stood sincere
I feel like a lucky little girl
Who must constantly play
Who must constantly whirl
I want the fame and fortune
For the reasons of thee
To always give of my heart
And live life according to me
To always keep learning
To love unconditionally is a yearning
To make my dreams real
Is an innate burning
Flames that are raging
With purpose and passion

To succeed for myself

In an orderly fashion

To take who I am

And stand proud and stand tall

To listen to my heart and mind in sync

And welcome it all

To travel to find

Some more birds of my feather

To bask in the sunlight

Yet to tackle the stormy weather

To cascade from the darkness to the light

And to reach altering heights

To thank those beloved up above

For the capability to love

For the opportunity to live

And the insatiable need to always give

To accept my loved ones unconditionally for who
        they are

And to shine bright with all the other stars

Psalms 37:4: I delight myself in the Lord and He gives me the desires of my heart.

2003-2004

SARAI LONDON TAILOR RECEIVES COUNTY MENTAL HEALTH AWARD

Congratulations to Sarai London Tailor of White Plains, a volunteer at New York Presbyterian Hospital, on receiving the Westchester County Department of Community Mental Health Award. Each year, the county honors a select group of Westchester residents for the time and energy they devote to improving the quality of life for their neighbors.

Ms. Tailor teaches patient education classes on mental dis-ease, illness, and treatment. She also serves as a member of the Consumer Advisory Committee. As a teacher, she is energetic and creates a trusting atmosphere for her students. As a committee member, she is a strong advocate for improvements in the hospital system, Ms. Tailor is persistent and does not shy away from conflict. She is well respected and an extremely valuable advisor and teacher for the hospital administration.

The Annual Awards Program was established by the Community Services Board of the Westchester County Department of Community Mental Health in 1982 to give special recognition to those who have made extraordinary efforts in the area of mental health.

Thank you, Sarai, for all your hard work!

Phillippians 4:12 I know both how to be abased and I know how to abound. Everywhere, and in all things, I am instructed both to be full and to be hungry, both to abound and to suffer need.

4:14 Notwithstanding, ye have well done that ye did communicate with my affection

Omnia Vincit Amour

Omnia Vincit Amour

Love is what it is for
It comes from our core
All things love travels from above
Encircling white doves
We must learn to wholeheartedly give
Then we shall master how to live
Give and take
Keeping it genuine and not fake
Can you imagine a world filled with peace?
Where there is less anguish and suffering for those
       that become deceased.

The Kingdom will be flabbergasted and gaping the
       word now
Splendor in the grass
Glory in the hour
Strip the devious devil of all of his evil power

Benevolence will prevail!
On the waterways we will sail!
On the learjets we will fly
To altitudes that are extremely high.
All the wounded birds will again fly

On ground we as a nation will stand proud
shouting and screaming in joy and celebration
   aloud.

This is holy fate
Open and run through the Holy Gates
We must no longer wait
There is a clear cut date
The time for redemption
And resurrection is now
Everyone onstage and in the audience deserves to
take a bow
We must be released from the leopards in our
   mind's cage
To live laugh and love to be free
And awaken to this utopia we see

The Blood Stained, Tainted Heart

God, heal me.

Heal in me whatever You see needs healing.

Heal me of whatever might separate me
   from You.

Heal my memory, heal my heart,

Heal my emotions, heal my spirit,

Heal my body, and heal my soul.

Lay your hands gently upon me

And heal me through your love for me.

    Being reborn in the light,

    No longer terrorized by the fright.

    Here for a certain mission,

    Finished with hospital readmissions.

    The sunlight reflects off my tired
       flesh,

    Wanting to be involved in helping
       humans

    And be enmeshed.

    May my God shine His stars on

    All of us. This must be a must.

The last days have come to
fruition. I have my petition,
Petition for happiness, peace, and
love. I draw all my strength from the
Angels from up above.

Reality Sweeps In

Wake up! Stop sleepwalking
and being suitably unconscious.
We are in the last days.
No longer a haunting haze.
It's a revelation, a new beginning, a whole
　　　new phase.
We no longer have to face the Rapture:
will we be able to capture a new holy
　　　beginning
while we keep sinning?

Resilient, brilliant, new developments
No resentments
More opportunities and sentiments.
Each one of us covered by the armor
　　　of the Trinity Sword
Blessed to be here in Utopia, on God's green
　　　earth.
To better serve the higher power of our

        choosing,

for all, the Lord.

To point towards rebirth.

Learning, changing, growing

no more self-worth of daily reaching

for one's stable girth.

What the World Needs Now

Lead back to the promised land.

Floating free on the dead sea

And part the red sand. Peace in Israel is to

    be real.

Those inflicted with pain and suffering will

    heal.

Revelation 21:4: the world will finally even

    the sorcerer's score.

We will each get to our heart's, spirit's, and

    mind's   core.

Core beliefs that, as a universe, we will lead

    back to

What was promised—

Great relief.

Utopia, noun: a state of the universe in

    balance and sync;

A peaceful and loving way to think.

The number thirty three, an example of

     Jesus prophesying love.

Healing and redemption without exemption.

Where each person who surrenders receives

     this glorified spirit.

A miraculous, unexplainable rebirth

Where each human has overflowing purpose

     and worth.

Euphoria, noun: a state of being happily elated with the use of illicit, mind-altering substances relinquished and faded.

Church Chat

At long last, it was the second coming of Christ. Yet, how could He literally come if it was the immaculate conception? It depends on how you view the filth yet wonder of semen; it surely is the biblical time to cast out your demons.

I pledge allegiance to the flag of the United States of America and to the republic for which it stands. One nation under God, indivisible, with liberty and justice for all.

Why has it become, over the centuries, one universe under God—invisible to all, small or tall?

Must we all fall? We could be standing one world under the staff and rod, praying to the one God.

Jubilation, exhilaration, even during trials of persecution and tribulation.

Experiencing all the five senses is the consequence, feeling a well of elation.

Some unfortunate souls have been battered and abused. They are guarded against affection and touch. All this is too much for them to endure. How much more must they take before they forgive and realize it wasn't their fault? It was a sadistic mistake!

The taste and spice of life. So many flavors to savor. Make sure you get your pieces of pie. Never stop reaching through the adjourning of darkness into the morning of periwinkle sky. Make sure you are spiritually nourished so all including yourself will continue to flourish.

Smell the fragrance of the regal flowers. They are sweet, not sour. Saturate them in baptismal water. Never let them die. As creatures on earth, as part of our nature, we are all moving at our own pace—growing—often wondering why.

Every moment, use your sight. Take the blindfolds off. Be afraid no longer of the devious devil's fright. Learn with each step more and more insight.

Sometimes as humans, we hear only what we want to hear. If we study and hear the bible's words,

why do some of us go into secular society and act absurd? We are rude to our brothers and sisters, fathers and mothers. We are rude to those that don't share our godly beliefs. We show them no mercy, patience, or relief. We think there is only one way to the divinity of the heavenly gate. Is that our fallacious fate?

No more of a cross to bear because Jesus will return and arrive safely. So we can forgo our overwhelming fear.

For you have heard of my previous way of life in Judaism, how intensely I persecuted the church of God and tried to destroy it. I was advancing in Judaism beyond many of my own age among my people and was extremely zealous for the traditions of my fathers. But when God, who set me apart from my mother's womb and called me by his grace, was pleased to reveal his Son in me so that I might preach him among the Gentiles, my immediate response was not to consult any human being. I did not go up to Jerusalem to see those who were apostles before I was, but I went into Arabia. Later I returned to Damascus. --Galatians 1:13-17

Now I say, That the heir, as long as he is a child, differeth nothing from a servant, though he be lord

of all; But is under tutors and governors until the time appointed of the father. Even so we, when we were children, were in bondage under the elements of the world: but when the fullness of the time was come, God sent forth his Son, made of a woman, made under the law, to redeem them that were under the law, that we might receive the adoption of sons. And because ye are sons, God hath sent forth the Spirit of his Son into your hearts, crying, Abba, Father. Wherefore thou art no more a servant, but a son; and if a son, then an heir of God through Christ.
--Galatians 4:1-7

Wi-Fi/Why? High-Sigh/Lie?

Are we losing reality at an information intersection? Buried in texting, social media, screens with blue-spectrum light blaring. No sleep—no time to talk to your family at the table. Headphones to muffle the music of everyday conversation. In trying to block out the crazy, we lose so much good; get so socially lazy. For years it's festered—as the connectivity increases, our vitality as a nation decreases.

Poor communication permuted at every level of the family. Brothers not talking to sisters. Parents divorcing at rates unheard of. Monogamy is a rare concept it seems most people cannot endure. Our faces stuck on our phones and our phones buried in our souls. When can we unblock God's number?

If we did, maybe we wouldn't be distracted by all of our debt, demoralized relationships, drained desires of what we used to think our life could be. Maybe the recession could be solvable if elected officials would open dialogue but how could that happen if we can't even talk?

And without that basis in understanding simple, common problems, how could we dare tackle that holy mackerel problem of those that can't speak for themselves? The homeless and the chemically-dependent; those with problems so large they often feel the nightmare of day-to-day rings endless?

When will we unite? When will we be courageous enough to spread insight? When will the darkness end and give way to God's everlasting light? Or are we only interested in promoting our websites? Homeless people in shelters are lying barely clothed on the littered concrete ground. One in five inflicted souls in America suffer from some variation of mental disease. The majority may never get better. Those not directly affected continue to turn away. It will destroy our world and take a terrible toll. Universal diseases are growing like wildfire. Are we possibly reaping what we are sowing? This answer is strictly for the Almighty, the All Knowing.

It's time to gather in a stampede. Not to impede, rather to succeed. To move gloriously forward, to lead; to make it a mission that we will feed the mouths and take care of the needs of underprivileged adults and kids. The difference between righteousness and victory is the significance.

Connect to the world through sharing your heart, spirit, and mind. And essentially, ultimately, and eternally, its reconstruction, resurrection, and recovery you will find!

Up in Harms

Bearing arms is part of the constitution,
Yet not knowing the least of baring souls
Leaves in our universe an abundance of
    death
And a gaping hole.

ISIS, the terrorist suicide bombers of a crisis
Because those that don't understand the
    loving,
healing, peaceful teachings of Christ
Or the other prophets--remain seekers of
    sorrows
Living dark tomorrows.

Christ was and will come again.
The only aching question is when.
When will all this violence, bigotry, and
    hatred end?

When as humans, under one God,
Will we become friends?
The abomination and ruination
of our nation on 9/11.
Those murdered were surely welcome into
    heaven.

Osama Sin Laden, responsible for roughly
    3,000 innocent lives
Put through mankind's hell,
Without a say, they unjustly fell to their

demise.
We will eternally mourn and cry.
We are in a new era or perhaps an error.
There is so much uncertainty and terror.
Once again, it is a Wi-Fi/Lie, High-Sigh/Lie.

It was Out of this World

Checking in only to check out.

It was the holiday season. The trees were shimmering with lights, ornaments, and wrapped presents. I wondered if I still would have a presence where I was headed. I lay in bed with excruciating pain from a newly discovered ulcer. The cocktail of pain pills, alcohol, and psychiatric meds took me to an alternate universe. It was out of this world. I became so detached from humanity and reality. I reluctantly believed I was the deplorable, disgusting, demonic, devious Devil. And I was petrified to leave my bed for fear that my neighbors would throw me into the gated community's gates of Hell. My apartment number was 4L and I thought it stood for Lucifer. The gate code was 999 and I truly believed that meant 666 backwards. I was trembling and, each time the phone rang, I thought the recipient was scorching me. I could dismiss going for ECT—electroconvulsive shock treatment.

I felt it should have been called Electric Convulsion *Shocking* Treatment.

Once I was released, I would do the circuit and end up in three more hospitals within a six month period. I know your social life can decrease as you get older, but I had to come up with better outlets, options, and hobbies than checking into psychiatric wards only to check out. Once I left the hospital, I faced being homeless. I was living in a luxurious apartment for many years and, sadly, ran out of funds. My only option was to move into the YWCA low-income housing. I guessed the days of living lifestyles of the rich and infamous had horrendously halted. I went from the penthouse living to the basement. It was a sad reality. Most of them would spend the days outside picking up cigarette butts off the ground or out of the garbage and smoking them. Yet I had so much empathy because each soul had a heart wrenching story about how they ended up living at the YWCA, including myself. How would I adjust from living with full amenities to living in a room the size of a shoebox with one small window, almost comparable to a jail cell? How would I give up frequent visits to five star restaurants? Eating Blue Point oysters on the half shell or going to Peter Luger's Steakhouse for a medium rare experience became surviving on food stamps and a weekly food pantry. I went from a life full of amenities to a life full of inequalities. At one point, I put all my money into a fidelity account. In today's uncertain world, I would've been more successful putting it in an infidelity account.

It was now Thanksgiving and I pondered what I had to be thankful for. Once again, the serpent had me wrapped around his middle finger. I wasn't strong enough to say, *go to your inflammable cage in Hell*. I had stopped taking my meds three months prior and was put back on them. I was starting to have peculiar thoughts and the demon of depression set in. My mother picked me up to go to my brother and sister-in-law's for the holiday. I was completely disheveled; hadn't showered, brushed my teeth, or shaved my legs and underarms in God only knows how long. And quite frankly, readers, I don't know you yet well enough to come clean. My poor mother was so upset. She screamed that she was such a good person that she didn't deserve this. I should be able to be responsible for taking care of my mental illness. She said she was done. If I wanted to spend the rest of my life in a mental institution, that was my choice. My mother would no longer visit me. I sat there silent as if they had done an emergency lobotomy. My mind short circuited. All I wanted to do was wake up from this nightmare. My every breath had been hijacked by mental illness. As the days progressed, my condition drastically declined. I was contemplating suicide again and sent my mother and dear friend some bizarre texts.

"I have finally realized and admitted the truth of how out of my mind I am and have always been. I am useless, repulsive, disgusting, crazy, inhumane, anti-social, ungodly, disconnected, non-functioning, unloving, unemotional. I am not fit for society. I deserve to suffer. I am a waste of human life. I have done nothing with the opportunities I have been given. I have caused nothing but pain and embarrassment. You were right, Mom, I don't deserve you. My life consists of laying in bed, staring at the TV, drinking iced coffees, smoking, and being in hospitals. I am so removed from the planet. I despise myself and I know you do too. You are such a beautiful person that hopefully you will be able to forgive me. Am I finally being honest, accurate."

My mother responded.

"Sarai, go no further with this self pity. I deleted all of it. If you can be honest and take your meds, go for ECT treatment, attend the program, and face your fears. Face everything and recover or forget everything and relapse. I am always in your corner. If not, I cannot be subjected to this anymore. It's really that simple. I love you now and forever. Pull yourself out of this black hole by doing what

you should even if it means forcing yourself.
You're a beautiful person, now act like one."

"There is no hope or answer. I have been
like this for a long time. Like you said, it's like a
broken record. I have no friends or family. No
feeling or thoughts, no abilities to talk or think. I
don't know how to be around anyone. The only
time I can function is when I am sleeping in silence.
There is nothing beautiful about me and I will burn
in Hell. Even with meds, program, and ECT, this is
reality. I wish I could disappear. Every minute feels
like an eternity with Satan."

I was completely disconnected from my
sweet Savior and have no control over these hang-
ups. For Christ's sake, I already had enough hang
ups of my own. My spiritual mentor and dear friend
who as a believer in Christ and the Holy Grail came
to do an exorcism to release my suffocating soul
from the penetrating, pathetic, and piercing pit of
Hell. She spoke to me in tongues I never understood

because each of us only has one tongue. Was I to be locked away for complete and utter insanity? Yet I can do all things through Christ who strengthens me. I needed more than a morning smoothie and B12 vitamin to bring me back to the light of day. I needed the blindfold to be removed so I could prevail over the empty, silent, darkness I had dove

into. I was sending disjointed messages and
thoughts out to those who loved me.

I already tried to take my life once and was
left with a permanent disability.

Text to spiritual mentor.

After speaking to Donna everyday
I hadn't heard from her.

Why haven't I heard from you?

Are you mad at me, repulsed,

Ashamed, embarrassed, tired?

Do you want nothing to do with me.

Am I a waste of life?

Why am I so sick and crazy

So detached from humanity?

Where am I going to end up?

There is no place for me.

The only place left for me was back to Hotel N.Y. Presbyterian. This was the reservation regardless of my reservations, elations, or sensations. The next time I called for a bed, it was going to be at the Hilton, not Motel 666.

Medical Records

██████████Medical Center

████████ Hospital ██████████ Division

ASSESSMENT   HOSPITAL

ADMISSION 2014

     TAILOR, SARAI L.

Assessment Date: 01/08/2014 9:50 PM

Discharge Summary

So sorry to be perverse or vulgar.

It's my symptoms acting up and out.

Perhaps I should have seen a gynecologist instead

of a psychiatrist or psychologist.

Next time I will try elopement risk of escaping. At

least I will get closer to marriage at 42 years of

age. Perhaps I will find myself a life-long spouse,

since I no longer think of myself as a complete and utter spouse.

CHIEF COMPLAINT/REASON FOR REFERRAL
Pt reports that she is agitated
HISTORY OF PRESENT ILLNESS

42 y.o single unemployed Caucasian female having a relapse of her bipolar d/o referred by wph cdt, with symptoms of irritability, psychomotorically agitated, explosive, distracted, grandiose with paranoid ideas that police are coming into her home and abducting her, also referring to the devil..Pt has a hx of impulsive suicide attempts and she may also be drinking.

Precipitants; Confusion, causing partial compliance of meds. Pt recently-12/1 /14 until 12/26/14 hospitalized but no ECT given. ECT has been helpful during acute decompensation in past. Lithium level 1/8/15 in AM was 1.8-pt received 2L

NS and Lithium level was rechecked at 5:02pm and was 1.07

From admission May 2014; Patient is a 42 y/o F with bipolar d/o and likely axis II pathology, currently in treatment at WPH CDT program, who was brought into WPH by her therapist at her program for worsening mania s/p ECT the last 2 years and feels like she is increasingly irritable. Has PMA, is explosive, distractible, grandiose, paranoid and thought disordered.

She states that "the people in my life are scared that I am getting too high, that I might be shot like Kennedy. I have to talk in riddles and rhymes." She is highly inappropriate throughout the interview, complimenting me and asking me intrusive personal questions. She is grandiose, irritable, labile, with flight of ideas. She plays a v/m from her psychiatrist then becomes paranoid that the room is wired and that he will hear her say this. She states that she has meetings with restaurant owners, copywriters, real estate agents so she is agreeable to stay but she wants to "get this party started as soon as possible."

Unclear if pt has been taking her medications

Name: TAILOR, SARAI L.

Functioning for the program. Pt was on risperdal and Wellbutrin, with monthly ECT, for the two years.

Beginning in Dec 13, pt began to refuse her meds, and also requested that ECt be spaced by 5 weeks. During this time, she was drinking with her roommate who got a DWI. Pt was admitted to hospital in 1/14, for depression, they did 3 x week ECT. She was readmitted to hospital in 3/14. This time, MD thought she was Axis 2 mostly, therapist found her to be psychotic and paranoid after discharge. In 4/14, pt made a suicide attempt by OD on her hoarded wellbutrin and risperdal. She was admitted to hospital, and discharged with no meds, MD there did not think she was psychotic, and that she was at risk for another OD. IN the last two weeks, pt has been coming to program, in a manic and disruptive. Yesterday, she got ECT, arrived at program out of control.

Therapist could not tell me why this pt is not on mood stabilizers.

We saw this pt in 2007, for intake, she was already getting ECT, and there is an entry that there was an adverse rxn to lithium, no details.

Additional info is that pt lost 100 lbs s/p bypass."

Pt and mother did not recall any adverse reaction to lithium. pt was treated with lithium and with risperdal. There was a gradual improvement, as the dose was titrated. behavior became more in control, mania subsided, psychosis remitted.

Pt was able to tolerate a whole day transition back to the CDT. At discharge, pt was much more stable, with no psychosis, no si/hi.

CONDITION UPON DISCHARGE

much improved

LIVING ARRANGEMENT AND AFTERCARE

own home

CDT

DISCHARGE MEDICATIONS/PRESCRIPTIONS GIVEN/INDICATIONS FOR USE 30 days:

risperdal 3mg po qam and hs - bipolar disorder

To be or not to be bipolar, that was my question. To live or not to live, that was my confusion. To choose peace and happiness, that was my answer.

Tailor, Sarai London

ADM DATE: 12/14/2015

43 y/o F

DOB: 1/10/1972

DISCHARGE DATE:

1/8/2016

DISCHARGE SUMMARY

Discharge date: 1/08/2016

History of Present Psychiatric Illness

As per the psychiatric assessment dated 12/14/2015: "Chief Complaint: 'I had crazy thoughts,' &. Pt is a 43 yo Caucasian female, domiciled with mother, unemployed on disability, with pmhx of drop foot, s/p gastric bypass, with no legal hx, no hx of violence, PPHX of bipolar type, multiple previous hospitalizations (>15 most recent in IN ZHH), OD on seroquel 8 years ago resulted in compartment syndrome and left foot drop. She stated that on Thanksgiving she had a "panic attack" in the context of paranoia being around people and then rapidly decompensated developing increasing paranoia, especially paranoia that people would think she was bad, religious delusions including thinking she was on fire because she was possessed by the Devil. She stated to her mother that she was dispensing her meds but when the mother went out patient entered mother's room and got all the pills. She was found unconscious and seizing by her mother. On admission to ED her Li level was 3.87. Clozaril total level 4365 and VPA level of 51.9. On arrival to the unit the patient was pleasant and cooperative. She reported her mood as flat and stated that while both the paranoia and delusions have decreased, they are still present. She stated that at this time she knows these things are not real. She reported her mood as "flat", denied SI/HI/i/p, VH, manic symptoms. She reported no change in sleep or appetite. She wants to Pt denies hx of substance abuse but reports smoking 1 ½ PPD. She reported Clozapine has "worked best so far."

Course of Treatment General/Medication Course: Please note that patient is on Assisted Outpatient Therapy. Writer observed that although patient had been placed on two medications that are generally thought to be suicide protective (lithium and clozapine), she actually used these in attempts twice in the last year. She also has a previous history of suicide attempts that resulted in compartment syndrome. Given her proclivity for suicide by overdose, it made sense to treat her with a long acting injectable medication and to limit her exposure to oral medication. She had a history of good response to risperdal and writer was able to confirm that long acting invega sustenna would be covered by her insurance for bipolar disorder with an approximate three dollar and sixty cent copay. She was therefore given a trial of oral invega for tolerance and effect. As per my first MSE with her on 12/15/2015, patient was acutely manic and psychotic: she is up and about, gait intact with a mild limp. She is unusually bright and active. She later lies alluringly in her bed, makes remarks about doctor "sweeping me off my feet," voice and production. Idealization. Denies SI/HI intents or plans but believes she is the Devil. Thought process tangential. Speech increased rate. Mood "good," affect extremely elevated and inappropriate. Judgment and insight are limited. Impulse control likely poor. She also had poor sleep. As her invega was titrated she slowly improved. Consistently denies SI/HI intents or plans from start. Her delusional thoughts and hallucinations attenuated at most an overly increased interest in religion which she could discuss appropriately and become less salient. Her thought process and verbal production also improved. Her affect remains mildly elevated and she jokes frequently but can be redirected. She is future oriented.

She received her first invega sustenna injection (156mg) on 12/23/2015 while she was receiving invega 9mg. She apparently developed some EPS (writer was on vacation, coverage reports) and was started on cogentin one mg twice daily which resolved with the cogentin and cessation of oral invega. She received the second dose of invega sustenna 156mg on 12/30/2015. She used sleep aides including initially trazodone for sleep. She attributed her sleeping problems to the noise on the unit and this may be true but I have my suspicions. In any event her sleep did improve and she did not require sleep aids every night. I cross tapered her from trazodone to Benadryl 150mg at bedtime and she reported she would not need Benadryl at home.

We discussed obtaining it OTC if needed and we also discussed, as she was aware, that it also could be used in a suicide attempt, as could her cogentin. In any event, though somewhat hypomanic, she is not an acute danger to herself or others. There are sleep considerations above and also the fact that she will be living with her mother who seems somewhat stressed by Surai's behavior. Surai's care management team is completing an HRA for her so that she can eventually move out of her mother's home. Please consider increasing her next dose of invega sustenna IM to something greater than 156mg q four weeks. She came from LIJ medicine with a slight wound on her right wrist which appears to be a burn. We discussed medicine and plastic surgery. It appears to be an eschar. She received silvadene cream and then later bacitracin for the wound. Home care services will continue to monitor the wound and patient is aware it will likely scar. No interventions are required so long as there are no complications such as infection. Instructed patient to apply bacitracin to the wound daily. She also receives parachute services to assist in her transition from inpatient hospital. AOT is aware of plan to discharge to partial hospital with expected later transition to her PROS program.

Relapse Prevention Worksheet: Reactions, Distractions, Attractions, and Relations

1. How can you recognize a sign that you are being triggered?

> When I am exposed to anxiety and stress. Big shopping areas, public transport, when things are not perfect.
>
> When I am going through a transition, whether good or bad. Fear of change is still evident.
>
> When I start having unrealistic visions and racing thoughts with theological connotations. Such as the idea that I am the Devil and responsible for all evil on Earth. Or that I am being persecuted and crucified by the Devil. If I don't try to break this

psychosis in its early stages, it has led to suicide attempts.

2. What are some physical or bodily reactions that you notice when you are not feeling well?

I am unable to achieve or maintain my ADL's (activities of daily living). I have no motivation to take care of myself in the high manner to which I have become accustomed. I am not able to practice proper hygiene in the least, I don't shower, shave, or wash and brush my hair. I don't do laundry or wear clean clothes. I look and feel completely unclean.

3. What are some emotions you experience during a difficult time?

I am comfortably numb, like Pink Floyd phrases it. My emotions have flatlined. I am not in touch with the beautiful, yet complex, feelings God gives to us. I feel like a cell phone when the tower goes down.

4. <u>What was one of the worst experiences you had while having symptoms?</u>

When I get terrible psychosis, or the dragon of severe depression breathes fire on me, I am too paranoid to tell anyone for fear of being ashamed, embarrassed, and being locked up in a state hospital for the rest of my days, until the bleak walls and ceilings cave in on me. During my last suicide attempt, my mom found me in her apartment convulsing, vomiting, urinating, and unconscious. I lay in a coma for four days in the ICU with my mom holding my hand and praying. She brought me the cutest Rudolph the Reindeer stuffed animal. I was intubated with a long tube and, miraculously, on the fourth day I was raised back to life like Lazarus. My tombstone would remain blank, thank God. I made a vow never to put my beautiful mother through that again. She said when she almost found me dead it was the worst day of her life, besides the day Dad died. From this point forward, if my symptoms returned, I would tell my family, trusted friends, and healthcare providers.

Never again would I try to tackle this offensive running back. Especially since I gave my life to Emmanuel, the Lord. I know I am not alone and I will be protected from the atrocities and criminal injustices of mental illness.

5. <u>List all coping mechanisms learned in treatment</u>

I like to refer to it as "coping though hoping."

- Be honest with your healthcare providers, such as psychiatrists and therapists about symptoms and feelings. Don't allow fear, shame, and embarrassment to take you down a slippery slope.
- Establish a healthy, loving support network and relationships. Rid yourself, even if it's slowly, of negative, toxic people.
- Don't isolate yourself. Try to keep socially engaged on any level you are comfortable with.
- Have a regular, consistent sleep pattern.
- Keep a routine or structure, whether it be a treatment program, volunteering,

working, or participating in your hobbies.

- Develop hobbies and passions. Be willing to try new things and explore options.
- Practice mindfulness, living, and savoring the moment. Don't allow yourself to be held captive to your past or be so fearful of your future that you remain stagnant.
- Stay compliant with medication and discuss adverse side effects with your doctor.
- Be a visionary. Envision goals you want to accomplish. Break them down to baby steps.
- Use exercise to release endorphins and reduce anxiety and stress.
- Try to eat healthy and in moderation. Be cognizant of portion control.
- Practice self care and self love, such as indulging in hygiene. Take long hot or cold showers—whichever you prefer. Enjoy bubble baths, massages, manicures and pedicures, facials. Whatever makes you feel good.
- For those of you that have a strong spiritual and faith component, continually learn about your faith and

work hard at not only believing in it, but developing it.

- Use meditation, yoga, deep breathing, or guided meditation where you are helped to a serene place such as a beach or a nature scenario. Meditation, elevation, and relaxation are good methods to live by.

- Use the arts as a means of healing and being in touch with your emotions and childlike essence, such as writing; whether it be keeping a diary, poetry, stories, or mere thoughts. Listening to music, try not to limit yourself to one genre. Painting, singing, coloring, dancing, acting. If none of those call to your soul, try and measure where you are using your creative abilities.

- Take time to have your "moment in the sun." Do it in moderation, due to the health risks of overexposure. Vitamin D, or Divine as I call it, is good for mind, body, and spirit.

- Lastly, and perhaps most important during difficult times, symptoms, or recurrences of illness or addiction, be gentle and patient with yourself. Put the bat down, so to speak. Take one inch, one step, one day at a time. And remember, "this, too, shall pass."

Angel Number 44

Ms. Sarai London Tailor
Born January 10th, 1972

The number forty four carries the doubled variations of the number four, making its energies and influences magnified. Number four resonates with the attributes of support and stability; establishing solid foundations for the self and others, willpower and effort, ability and worthiness, hard work and success, wholeness and inner wisdom. Four is associated with our passions and drive and the energies of the Archangels .

Angel Number Forty Four asks that you pay attention to your intuition and inner wisdom, as your connection with your angels and the angelic realm is very strong at this time. You are encouraged to continue on your current path, as your drive and determination will lead you to success and fulfillment.

Angel Number Forty Four brings the message that you are surrounded by helpful, loving angels who wish to bring you peace of mind and joy of heart. Angel Number Forty Four indicates that you are being given support and encouragement along with your path and, when faced with an obstacle, rest assured that your angels are more than willing to assist. Be assured that solutions to any issues or problems will soon be revealed.

Angel Number Forty Four is a message that the angels and Archangels are with you, encouraging and guiding you. They are offering you inner strength and support to enable you to get the work done that you need to in order to achieve your goals and aspirations. They understand you have been toiling diligently towards them and encourage you to continue on your current path to achieve the results you desire. Work with the angels to ensure success in all your endeavors.

Angel Number Forty Four tells you that you have nothing to fear in regards to your life, work, and the divine purpose and soul mission. The angels surround you, encouraging you to keep up the good work. The Archangels are always available for help and guidance—all you need to do is ask.

Rise to the Occasion

Jesus turned thirty three.
This was when we were all set from the shackles
　　free.
No more bondage of one's own;
We will be able to speak the truth
With a proper, steady tone.
No more the life sentence of existing alone.
He will rise from His death.
Each one of us will victoriously live out the day
with each earthly breath—
No longer a dreamlike phase.
In reality learning and using new ways
One moment, one day at a time, spending days
Perfecting how to act and what to say.
Remove Jesus from the cross.
Soothe Him and let Him peacefully lay.
Let us be pain and sin free,
Honor who we will become and be.
With this reality, we are all wealthy enough;
There will be no monetary fee.
Play your anointed role well.
Always have much to learn and to tell.
Shine like a sparkling eternal star.
Go far using faith and resilience.
Set your standard on a high bar.
Don't stay victim like

A bear that hibernates.
Happiness and peace of mind
Could be your fate.
What life did Jesus the savior give?
His spirit in each of us so we may live.

Welcome to the first days of the our last days...He's
        coming back.
Satan had me under attack—
My cold body lay on a hospital gurney in a gown.
I was not smiling, rather had a fatalistic frown.
Fighting to rise from death,
Fighting for life's breath.
I had a breathing tube down my throat.
These could have been the last words I wrote.
I was in restraints,
Needed analysis,

Developed a blood clot—
I was dealing with an enormous lot.
In the emergency room, I had an out of body
        experience.
I believed the doctors had said they were planning
        for my funeral.
It was traumatic and surreal.
However, even though I was betrayed by mental
        illness and life
I rose again because my work for God was not
nearly done on earth.

It was an exhilarating rebirth!

When I opened my eyes, the doctors asked me if I
heard voices.
I heard the rejoicing of the angels
And finally felt I had heard the voice of reason from
my Messiah, Jesus.
I knew deep in my soul I would be an advocate and
activist for the mentally ill.
I would do my fair share;
I would have my fill.
No longer would I succumb to being dreary, leery,
nor weary.
I had risen beyond spiritual warfare;
The veil was no longer blindfolding me,
My eyes were bare.
I could conceive, believe, and achieve.
I knew the Devil was the culprit of cruelty, frailty,
brutality, and insanity.
However, it was my noble vow to join the stampede
of those who worshiped—
The tragic beauty of humanity and the majesty of
our crowned Father on earth.
Being a part of rather than apart from the kingdom
was true
purity, patience, perseverance, and self worth.

2 Timothy 1:7

For God hath not given us a spirit of fear,
but of power and of love
and sound mind

Redemption without Exemption

The gift of life
The daring of dreams
The desire for depth
The benevolence and joy of breath

The glow of the eyes' gleam
A preponderance of screams
Unite as spiritual warfare teams

Coming together under God's sun
Many changes for the better will be done
Wilted flowers rebloom
Firecrackers reboom
And all pure souls will be exhumed

The Real Deal

Was I, at long last, willing to take off the veil and layers of my mask? Was I engaged in introducing and revealing myself to the world as my authentic self? Was I ready and brave enough to play the role that my Creator had uniquely handcrafted for me? Was I willing to play it with humility, compassion, and God's ultimate strength? When I fell short in my capabilities, would I have the know-how and courage to reach out for the Lord and for his eternal abilities?

Greatest Weaknesses

1. The act of entanglement and smothering others. Infringing on people's personal space. Caring so much that I blur the lines and can't properly categorize people. I continuously work on proper and appropriate boundaries so I can sustain deep, meaningful relationships, as I believe this is the sustenance of life.

2. Loving too deeply and trusting others with my emotions easily. Putting loved ones on unrealistic pedestals only for them to fall. Exposing myself to others so greatly that— much of the time—I am let

down, taken advantage of, and disappointed to the point of having my heart broken.

3. Still being regretful, a little angry, and resentful that I was unable to have children due to the severity of my mental illness. I made a choice that I wouldn't become a mother unless I was able to follow the exceptional role model my own mother provided. I also didn't want to take the chance of genetically passing the mental illness on to my own child. However, perhaps all this was, in some way, more God's choice for my life path and something I would have to come to accept.

I am blessed to have three beautiful—inside and out—girls in my life that are like daughters to me. Isabella (Izzy B) is my little six year old fairy princess. Madzz is my rambunctious, astounding young lady to be and Lauren is my twenty six year old "Go to Girl." She is the first to see all the beauty and opportunity the world has to offer. The different ages of these dear girls provide me with different viewpoints and bring me back to the majority of my own memories and experiences. None of them were biologically conceived by me, yet neither was Jesus from the Virgin Mary. And their love was endearing, enduring, and everlasting.

Biggest Success

1. My resilience to constantly fight to come back from the pit holes of mental illness. I have been knocked down more times than Derek Jeter used his bat before retirement and, with a vengeance, I continually get up to do God's will and work. Perhaps because He gives you an enormous tax break for doing charitable causes.

2. The completion and publication of my books. After seven years of working on it, I finally can say with great joy that it is complete. My passion and perseverance to get the book to those believers and suffering souls to make a mountain of positive difference. May it be the ultimate revelation. "May the power of the tongue bring life, not death."

Regardless of how grandiose my life has presented at times, I pray with great fervor that I remain humble, compassionate, grateful, kind, open hearted, and open minded. Most of all, I pray that I am able to evoke peace, love, and happiness in myself and others.

God's Merci Beaucoup

My emotions were in place. I had a full range of expression. My creativity from the Creator was back. I was excited, enthused, and hopeful for each new moment, for each new day, to put all my worries away. And with everything I am, I pray. I had dismissed and buried the pain and misery of laying dirty in slothful sin in bed, in a vegetative state—emotionally removed. No longer contemplating giving the Devil power over my life, I was ready, willing, able. Thank you, Jesus; I was mentally and physically stable. Now, I can play my captivating role on the Paramount movie screen.

Amazing Face

How succulently sweet it is,
That saved a kvetch like me.
I once was drowning in a sea of darkness,
Now I am swimming full circle in lust for the light.
It's my time to be—
Restraints are off.
I'm finally on the wings of an angel.
I am fantabulously free;
Free from the jungle of havoc, chaos, persecution,
        and despair.
Finally existing in reality and self aware.
Do I reach out with my tiny hands
For the pinnacle? Do I dare?
God, grant me the serenity, the security, the safety
To accept the things I cannot alter,
The cou(rage) of the heart to change the things I can
And the wisdom to know the difference.
To veer away from indifference
And discern reverence. Amen!
Ah man/Ah woman!

*Taken from Bill W's 12 Step recovery program,
accompanied by Ms. Sarai London Tailor
        Curious George*

Christ paid the price.

It was all humanity's loss that devastating day on
the cross.

Yet, hopefully everyone realizes

God's in charge, he's the CEO—

The Big Boss.

See life through the curious

Eyes of a child of god and you will discover and
recover

A perpetual source of happiness and ecstasy.

You are cordially invited to

Be inquisitive about yourself and be

Interested in in other people and you

Will be granted and enchanted

And given a source

Of fascination—be cautious of procrastination.

We need time to analyze and search

For the answers and explore.

It is so illuminating that you will surely soar—

Learn always more. As a young child,

  I wanted to know, I wanted to grow,

  I wanted to reap, I wanted to sow.

1. Why, Mommie and Daddy, do I have to look both ways before I cross the street? Won't God just guide my feet?

2. Why can't I have more ice cream, candy, and play. Do I always have to listen to and agree to what you say?

3. Can I express my emotions in all different ways?

4. Why do I have to take classes in school that don't interest me when I already have a vision of, when I grow up, what I want to be?

5. Why do good people suffer so much grief and pain? Is that the true definition of insane?

6. Why can't everybody be my best friend? Why does the happiness I feel and exude have to come to a screeching end?

7. Why does the Bogeyman hold me captive in the night? Won't you, Mommie and Daddy, hold me tight?

8. Why do families, friends, and nations resort to anger and violence and fight? When will they discover peaceful insight?

9. Why are the blessings of birthdays and holidays only on the calendar once a year? That brings to my eyes many tears.

10. Why, when my father was terminally ill and dying, did I block out the pain and barricade myself in my room with constant crying?

As the years progressed, the questions at times regressed, yet became more lethal and transgressed.

11. Do you want to know and accept the truth? Does God really love us unconditionally? Will His presence on our path always be?

12. Will war and suffering ever end? Will love, strength, and peace defend?

13. What happens to our spiritual heart and soul when we perish?

14. Will we join the cherubs in heaven and be
cherished?

15. Is there any hope for those that conduct their
lives in a sinful way? Will they be redeemed and
forgiven? Do the unrighteous deserve their say?

16. For those that have a sexual identity crisis or are
gay, why is it society's place to harshly crucify?
This leaves me with an exhausting sigh!

17. Why, when some tortured victim takes their
own life, do we tell ourselves they've gone to hell?
That they automatically from the pedestal of purity
fell?

18. Why, when we become adults, is it perceived
that asking others questions about themselves is

being intrusive and inappropriate? Isn't this the way to stay connected and have our fires lit?

19. Why are so many people scared to share their life story? Why do some humans hide feverishly from the morning dew and God's glory?

20. Why do we constantly repeat negative events in our world? Why can't we together move towards utopia and be released from the capitalist spiral to be free?

21. Why is it His story and not Her story? Perhaps it's meant to be The Story. The book of Holy life has a space for every given name. Each unique individual claims their own purpose, acclaim, and level of fame.

With God in our lives, the answers to these puzzling questions become clairvoyant and more clear. We relinquish the fear, act more sincere, and to the Ten Commandments adhere!

It's Time to Play Ball and Step up to the Plate

It's the world theories
The angels versus the devils
Bases loaded
Batter up
Two strikes
Three strikes and you're a social outcast
Last licks
It's a grand slam
The angels are the champions amongst
champions and victorious
We are all sluggers in our own rights

Take me out to the ball game
Take me out to the crowd
Buy me some peanuts and Cracker Jacks
I don't care if I ever come back
For it's root root root
For the Heavenly Homecoming Team
I don't care what they say
For it's one two three strikes you're in
At the old soul game

USA: University of Self Awareness

Once upon a time, in a land so far away, there thrived the Angel of Awareness. Awareness is the epiphany of recovery. Recovering lost dreams from false hopes. Rediscovering the rhythm of savoring a moment of innocence. She would spread her wings so vastly that all the beautifully colored butterflies would emerge from their hard-shell cocoons and follow her in awe. With her flight, she would recite the lyrics so melodiously that all the soaring birds would gloriously chime in.

Redeem the Dream 33 is my book about just that—my battle with bipolar dis-ease; the laughs and the lowest points (sharing a jail cell) to impart a lesson that soothes the soul. The Angel of Awareness is a good friend to have. (The Jesus Christ Consciousness: he ministered for healing and redemption, was betrayed, crucified, yet rose again at age thirty three.) Each human who dares has the capacity to rise again. His message, His consciousness, taught humankind a life of forgiveness, selflessness, and the value of living life positively. What would He do? How would He temper His actions rather than reacting defensively, angrily, and abusively? Whatever belief each human is called to—as long as the path is benevolent, virtuous, and loving—all avenues lead to a peaceful being.

With a little help from the Angel's wand, when each person rids themselves of the pain of guilt, shame, and disappointment, they will come to know themselves as twinkling stars. Then what started out as a little star grows into a universal victory of brightness, empowerment, and unity.

I wasn't necessarily searching for the Angel or for stardom, just feverishly questing after the kingdom as a child of God.

God-ian Angels Among Us

I was lost, caged in the wilderness with the deceiving Devil. It was a blustery, cold day. Took a shortcut through the woods. And I was confused about my way. It was getting late and I was scared and alone. But then, a one of a kind soul took my hand and led me to a heavenly home.

Oh, I undoubtedly believe in my heart of all hearts there are God-ian Angels among us, from somewhere else up above. They come to you and me in our deepest, darkest hours to show us how to give and to unconditionally forgive. To guide us with the light of faith.

When life held troubled times and had me down and out on my knees, there's always been someone to come along; to console and comfort me. A kind compliment from a stranger to lend a helping hand. A phone call from a friend just to say I love you and I understand. Yet, isn't it kind of funny, at the dark detouring end of the road, that someone lights the way with just a single ray of hope.

Oh, I undoubtedly believe in my heart of all hearts that there are God-ian angels among us sent down to us from somewhere up above. They come to you and me in our deepest, darkest hours to show us how to give and to unconditionally forgive. To guide us with the light of faith.

They wear so many poker faces, show up in unknown places, to grace us with their mercy in our time of need.

Oh, I undoubtedly believe in my heart of all hearts that there are God-ian angels among us sent down to us from somewhere up above. They come to you and me in our deepest, darkest hours to show us how to give and to unconditionally forgive. To guide us with the light of faith.

By an unknown author accompanied by Ms. Sarai London Tailor

Mother's Day 2015

To my saintly, sweet Sophia,

There is nothing so great as a mother's love. It surpasses all the peace and purity of the uniquely different snowflakes and of the white doves. I will always hold steadfast to the time when you told me, "anything is attainable as long as you have breath." My respect and admiration for you has limitless depth. You're such a class act and that, my dear Sophia, is a fact.

Although you are a private and reserved individual, you are a magnificent, beautiful soul. I am so honored to call you my mother. Even during the difficult times, I would never choose another.

You have always taught me the essentials, lessons, and morals of life.

And thank God that you saw me through all my devastating strife. I am so sorry I exposed you to my suffering and pain. I had no choice. It was the mental illness and how it tricks you into believing you're insane.

I pray each day that the pain will remain far in the past. My love and gratitude towards you—from which my inspiration for writing this will now and forever last.

Always your "Lori Belle"
November 24th 2016

So Much to be Thankful For

Happy B-Day, my darling Mummie dearest!
I love you now and forever and that comes
from the
deepest part of my heart. It all began from the first
hello, from the start.
You cradled me and held me with such love.
I surely knew I was a lucky girl watched
from
above. I hit the jackpot, had a windfall, because
you, my beloved mother, I could call. The passing
hasn't always been good or kind or fair. Yet

together, as a team, we were able to overcome and
bear despair.

You are such a beautiful lady inside and out.
Even when you act obnoxious and shout.
I pray you will always be "horsing around"
for all the rest of your days on earth.

And you'll never forsake our incredible
connection, begun at birth.

You are the "Wind Beneath my Wings"
even though you get annoyed that I
constantly sing.
So stay your classy, inspiring self and may
this b-day, and all the rest that follow, shine
God's sun on you.

Always with all my love,
Your baby girl
Lori Belle

Testimonials

It was the spring of 2010, if memory serves me. A close girlfriend and I arranged to have lunch at a local hotspot restaurant by day and lounge bar by night. They have lovely outdoor seating on nice days and this was one of those days. We enjoyed a fabulous time, eating and chatting. Two ladies sitting behind us got up to use the restroom. As they walked past us, they noticed what we were eating. They commented on how lovely the place was and especially how delicious the food was. We laughed and commented that we agreed. After they returned and settled up their bill, they acknowledged us and went on their way.

My friend and I lingered a bit more and, eventually, we settled our bill, went to use the restroom. While we were in the restroom, we commented to each other how nice the two women were. It was a beautiful sunshiney day. We always enjoy each other's company and whenever we are together, great things seem to just happen around us, to us, and because of us. We always attributed it to our faith and belief in Christ and our general overall pleasant nature.

Now, my friend and I are fresh off this discussion and making our way to the parking lot. Not more than ten steps into the lot, the two friends we met are in a convertible with the top down. They wave to us and pull up. It felt like friends forever who just ran into each other all over again. We laughed and shared how nice it was to meet them.

We all exchanged information and promised to keep in touch.

Sarai and Lorna are two of the loveliest friends a girl could make. In fact, Sarai is responsible for referring me to her church, which I now lovingly refer to as my church. I was baptized there in 2012. Sarai is a blessing to everyone she meets. What a true blessing these two ladies have made in our lives. There are people in this life that come into your life...for a reason, a season or a lifetime. So nice when you meet the lifetime ones!

My friend asked me to write a quick accounting of how we met and I am so happy to be included in her new book. What an honor!

With love and blessings,

S.M.Z.

Sarai,

I think of you so often and when Mom said we haven't seen each other in ten years, I thought that couldn't possibly be true--impossible. There truly has never been any distance in my heart and my love for both of you.

Sadly, our challenges at times dictate the loss of precious time. We have shared quite a few special moments. You were always filled with wisdom. Your warm, loving heart surely shines. And that wit of yours and your laugh had me laughing out loud for sure. I don't know why such a struggle is placed in your life and I'm not sure we will ever fully understand. What I do know is you persevere, possess great strength and courage, and land on your feet each and every time. The world has asked a lot of you at times, but a world without you in it would be missing a bright light. Whether you know that or not, you stir our spirits, move our hearts, and help each of us who are blessed to know you. Listen more deeply to our life's purpose.

I have listened deeply to you, our talks always provided new found wisdom unanswered. For where would we be if we have no more questions?

The day you decided to call me Godmother, know I was honored. For I knew we shared the special little things that special friends do.

Words at times seem inadequate and inadequate I feel during this time. For always I wish I could do more or just carry part of your burden for you. Hey, wish I could pass along mine, too. Wouldn't that be easy? :)

I have been forced to learn patience. Be patient. This time will pass and you will discover something new in having the experience.

I have always and will always simply adore you, and if you ever need anything at all, I would come running.

I'm still writing. Hope you are, too. That's an incredible journey in itself. Rest. I'm thinking and praying for you.

Strong you are.

Love,

Linda

I first met my beautiful friend Sarai approximately fifteen years ago, which would have been the year 2000. Sarai and I met at a treatment center for those suffering with eating disorders. I was there for bulimia and she for compulsive overeating. Sarai and I hit it off immediately. She made me laugh and laugh and laugh. Sarai has an amazing sense of humor. We have stayed friends since treatment. Sarai lives in New York and I live in Florida, which prevents me from seeing her as much as we would like. One incident I remember that happened in treatment was we were supposed to be meditating in class. My head was touching Sarai's head as we were sitting with our bodies extending outward in different directions with our heads touching. All I can tell you is we did very little meditating as Sarai had a great sleep throughout the session. However, due to her incredible snoring, I could not get calm enough even if I was paid to. I loved Sarai so much then and continue to do so today. So all we could do was laugh about the experience. That is just what it was and is. Sarai and I would and could laugh about everything. Even through the tears of frustration and disappointments in life, we could end up smiling at each other with a huge hug.I believe Sarai and I met through God given intervention. At the time I met Sarai, she described herself as a Messianic Jew. I was brought up in a Jewish household. However, I was never instructed and encouraged to attend Hebrew school or temple except for bar mitzvahs. Growing up, I remember asking my mother and grandmother, "who was God?" Their explanation was, "we are still waiting for the Messiah." I do not ever remember having any discussion surrounding the word God. I knew my grandmother was brought up in an orthodox family and we were never to have dairy and meat together. If you asked me why at the time, I would not have had an answer for you. I knew my mother was very strict about dating outside the Jewish faith. Whenever I was very rebellious and really a Mother's Nightmare, my mother used to say, "I hope you have a daughter just like you." Well thank God, although I did not always feel this, God saw to it that I could not have children. Getting back to my point, I had many problems with alcohol and drugs and finally, after many attempts in treatment, I finally got sober in Alcoholics Anonymous. It was there that I found a God of my own understanding. At first I visualized a Santa Claus type man or a big grandfather looking type man. Then approximately two years ago, I was still doing my daily prayers as they taught me in AA. However, I began seeing a man with semi long, black hair and dark eyes and it brought me comfort. I saw this man every day up until today when I pray. I attended a Bible study at a friend's house and began reading the Bible for the first time. It was awesome!! During the Bible study I began attending St. Thomas Moore Catholic Church and joined the RCDIA Program they had. Which was for those who wished to convert from their current religion to Catholicism. I figured out it was Jesus I was praying to. When I pray, I know I am praying to Jesus, God, and the Holy Spirit. I have not figured it all out yet...I was conflicted for a time. However, with prayer, Bible study, and the church, I came to believe and understand. Although at times, I didn't. But as long as I try to the best of my ability to do His will I never have to understand—just love, be tolerant, caring, patient, honest, and sincere. I am not trying to say I'm like this all the time. However, I try to work on myself through the love of my God, His son Jesus, my friends, AA, and therapy. Some of us are sicker than others and need a lot of help. I have Multiple Sclerosis. However, I can walk, talk, breathe, pray, and love. What more could I ask for? I have a wonderful family and a wonderful friend named Sarai and I thank God every day for putting people like her into my life.

From my beloved, dear friend Bec, who I lost a few months after she composed this eloquent letter for the book. After a long, strength-filled battle with MS, she died at age 56. I will miss her unique, loving spirit each and every day. She added so much joy and enlightenment to my life! I know she is resting peacefully in the gentle yet strong arms of the Creator.

Christmas 2015 card

I'm wishing only
the best things for you.
Like hope—the kind that's real
and can't be shaken.
Smiles in unexpected places.
Strength to persevere when things get tough.
I'm wishing you days filled
with the kind of happiness
that never really goes away—
the kind that comes from knowing
you're surrounded by people who love,
believe in you,
and will always be there for you.
I'm wishing you love
that surrounds you all the time,
no matter where you are.

I'm wishing you all these things, and more,
because you're the kind of person who
deserves to be happy—
the kind of person who deserves only the
best.

Love,
Jessula & Rudy

My name is Kim M. and how I met my sweet friend Sarai London Tailor, Loribelle to her friends, began a few years ago in an outpatient program for people with adversities of mental illness to regroup, heal, and hopefully move onward. I, Kim, am the oldest daughter of seven children of a large Irish Catholic family. I take great pride in and love my seven siblings and my Irish heritage. Also, like my friend Sarai would tell you, I love to tell a good yarn a mile long. My friend Sarai entered the program I was already in and, upon meeting her, I warmed to her kindness and outgoing nature unusually fast for me. For though I am kind, I am opinionated and have been known to kick like an ornery mule in my own fashion. Especially when I believe something strongly. Sarai, too, can be similarly strong. Thank God. I can't connect otherwise. But it was her warmth and her heart that connected us so quickly. Soon, I was looking for her daily in the program and was quite sad if she was missing for the day. We were soon spending time out and about together and we began a series of fun chats over coffee that we affectionately dubbed our "coffee runs." The car became the "Sarai Mobile." That little VW Bug was our willing chariot. When the top went down, we enjoyed the sun on a nice day. I learned many things about Sarai: her dad's tragic passing at a young age, her food addiction, and her diagnoses with bipolar disorder and psychosis. The most important thing was that Sarai and I shared a love for Jesus. She was a converted "Jew for Jesus" and I, a lifelong Catholic. One incredible moment occurred when the radio in the "Sarai Mobile" played the song "The Great I Am" by Phillips, Craig, and Dean. Suddenly we were having a spiritual moment before the Lord Himself, belting out this incredible song together for the whole world to hear. Thank God Sarai was moved to sway her hands in the air and really impress Him! She was driving and the Spirit was driving her! For us, that moment was powerful and incredible as granite. We were now two women worshiping and serving our Lord and we were never the same again. I've played that song many times since, on my guitar and elsewhere, and it will always move me. It was so holy, tightly binding us as deep friends who felt a mission of sorts to love more and deeper somehow in life.

Much has happened since then. Sarai had to go through a lot of saddening situations and serious problems for the better part of the last two years. We were both going through so much change, as iron sharpens iron. We fought many hellish fires as we both endured recurrences and bouts of our mental dis-ease. My brother died, as did a friend of ours. Sarai struggled hard and fought back with both spiritual and material pains.

Yet, as Jesus is her captain and mine, He led us through personal and spiritual trials to safety. For a while, it drew us apart, affecting and testing our friendship. However, God regrouped and recuperated us both...For God promises to not let us be tested beyond our limits nor leave us orphans ever. His victory had every problem in His hands leading us still onward, still upward. For God, there is no time or space and, therefore, wherever we were or are or ever will be, we grew and are growing stronger as friends and as people. Sarai and I are supportive of one another during the peaks and valleys of life. My boyfriend Steven is a dear one who stands by me as well. Strong, smart, kind, and generous, like Sarai and myself. He fights for his goals despite having schizophrenia—a different mental illness than ours. He and I have been together for six years. Steve, Sarai, and I believe the secret for those suffering with mental illness in life and relationships, especially romantic ones, is a bit tricky. Don't look the gift horse of your loved ones and friends in the mouth, but fight instead with tenacity for your dreams. Be determined never to give up on the good. And love yourself and all as our Lord loves us, even if it hurts. Make Jesus your captain and, with the help of the Holy Trinity, you won't be sorry. God is mysterious; the lover of our souls. His ways are above ours.

Happiness, for me in the end, will be when all He promised to those that abide and hear Him. Sarai and

I will not be left behind. My sweet friend and I will wave out the window of the car as we drive joyfully through the pearly gates praising and proclaiming forever and ever: "Holy, holy, God Almighty who is worthy! The Great I Am." When our reward comes, as our Savior Jesus waves back at us as He now waves inside. Amen.

Love,
Kimme

2016

Happy B-day…May all your wildest dreams be yours and the Lord's!
My beautiful Prima Donna Bells, you have been a joy and one of my angels on Earth.
Not only have you redirected me to a rebirth, you've also taught me what it meant to take back my self worth.
With your illuminating, Jesus-induced light, you've wiped away my fears and fright.
You've also spread some incredible insight.
You are my shooting star; my eternal, dear friend come near or come far.
Every day that I am given breath I am thankful for your presence in my life. You helped me to decipher the blessings from the strife.
You've encouraged me to go after my dreams and that reality isn't as dark as it seems.
You are a true example of what a godly woman should be. Thanks to your belief in me, I am no longer in spiritual solitary

confinement; I am mindfully and gratefully free.

With all my love,
"Lori Belle"

One day at a time

One step at a time

You can make it!

Hope today is a very good day for you

Dearest Lori Belle,

Happy & healthy birthday & everyday!

You are an amazing person in all you do and all you
give to others. Beautiful inside and out—that's my
Sarai! Continue to allow our Lord to do His work
through you. The struggle and the warmth that He

will impart to you to live a pure and fulfilled life
with much joy & happiness—

All my love always,
Donna xoxo

Jan 10, 2016

Dearest Sarai,

Happy Birthday, you fabulous thing!

Happiest of birthdays today and always. You are a
beautiful girl (lady) inside and out! You have
blossomed and evolved into the woman God has
anointed for this special journey! I'm so proud of
your tenacious spirit. Never give up, the best is yet
to come. Your hard work and diligence has not been
in vain. (You're so vain! Lol!)

May you continue the walk, praising and thanking
Him daily. In His perfect time, all from our
wonderful Lord will come to fruition. Be patient,

press on, live life to the fullest every day. Be blessed today and forever.

All my love,
Donna

I met Sarai at a Messianic temple one
Shabbat evening in White Plains around 2005. That
night the rabbi asked if I would be interested in
having Sarai London Tailor as my disciple.

Who would ever say no? Sarai was gentle,
kind hearted, and eager to learn about Yeshua,
Jesus, the Messiah. Sarai needed to understand how
her Jewish roots intertwined with Jesus. Growing
up, most of us believed He was the God of the
gentiles and we were still waiting for the Jewish
Messiah. Truth be known, believing in Jesus has
completed this Jew because I was willing to accept
Him into my heart as the one and only King of
Kings, the Jewish Messiah of Israel. Sarai and I
began meeting and speaking together about Yeshua.
Then other events occurred. Once again, Sarai was
dealing with the challenges of her mental illness.
Since I had not been involved in her life for too
long at the time, we had a hiatus until 2010.

We built a close friendship at that point. We
were speaking on a spiritual level which bonded us
and manifested itself into a special women's
friendship; the kind where you share your heart and
secrets. I was there for Sarai, not only to teach her
about the word of God, but also to depend on and
trust Him with a deeper, greater magnitude. We
would pray together often. Sarai was beginning to
pray on her own. She needed to build spiritual
strength on her own. This would enable her to

conquer the demons that were lying to her. She could not allow them to impede her anymore! No more heartache! She needed to hold onto the Messiah with all her heart, soul, and mind. She was in the valley, unable to overcome her depression. Unfortunately, she was in and out of the hospital. This was a vicious cycle for her.

However, she wouldn't give up. God would give her the strength required to work and believe, then finally feel whole again. Sarai's desire to share and help others through her own painful experiences resurrected her will to thrive with passion for life once again. Her heart was set on showing others with mental illnesses that there is a true, bright light at the end of the tunnel. Her innermost desire throughout her book and life was to help others to not have to go through what she had to endure so painfully. Sarai and I were and are blessed to have built a friendship in the kingdom of God. I was privileged to have baptized her in my pool where we used to have days for God's children in fellowship to worship and get baptized.

Our fellowship evolved to a new level in 2011. I shared with Sarai that I was legally separated from my husband. I was concerned because we were her duo of friendship; a married couple in God. I knew I was letting her down! I had been living a lie to please my family; protecting my children and everyone else. Sarai was compassionate and understanding. She cried with me and looked to God for strength, obviously sad but knowing in the depths of her heart that she needed to be my friend unconditionally. The role Sarai was gaining in her walk with Yeshua was making her an amazing, beautiful friend. A faithful and valued believer to me now.

I'm very proud of my dear friend Sarai. I believe when you give God the control and become the copilot, your path and journey in life will become a lot more visible and it will be easier to attain peace and comfort.

> Sarai, may God bless you as you find your way!
> Love and blessings xoxo
> Donna

Tidings of Peace

I solemnly promise to tell the whole truth, nothing but the truth, so help me God. It is my utmost vow to change the face of humanity and its struggle with insanity from a frown to a majestic crown with each individual in droves moving toward the parliament of Heaven. I will be a teacher, a preacher, and—at times—a screecher with my loud, boisterous, yet melodious voice. I will never have the magnitude of the **Mighty Prince of Peace**. Yet I would be content as a grassroots Jewish American Prince-ass of Peace, as my mother lovingly teases.

Wherever my magic carpet ride continues to take me, it is essential to remember that—although life can be tragically beautiful—I have been blessed beyond belief. I will never succumb to the low man on the bottom. Yet, even if I reach the top of Mt. Everest or Mt. Masada, I am no better nor worse than any wandering Jew that came before me or after. I am merely a human being, *being* the woman that God uniquely designed. I am following my dreams "somewhere over the rainbow" into everlasting fields of evergreen.

However, the Lord needs each one of us to do our part to recreate this somewhat frail, frigid world. He's in problem solving meetings all day and all night long. He is having meetings about meetings for our lack of free will participation. The Savior is desperately trying to accommodate everyone's prayers.

Matthew 6:10 Thy kingdom come, Thy will be done on earth, as it is in heaven.

Psalm 45 My heart is indicating a good matter: I speak of the things which I have made touching the King: my tongue is the pen of a ready writer.

4-24-2017

My Mummie Dearest,

I love you now and forever from here to eternity. For today, yesterday, and tomorrow. Thank you for always being an inspiration to me and giving me so much hope!

Always,
Your Lori Belle

Rev Me Up 33 (Eternity)

Volume Three

By Sarai London Tailor

aka Ms. Lori Eve Tatarsky

Rev Me Up 33
(Eternity)

I shall give fully and openly my heart to the world. Shall the world, in return, give its heart to me? I shall live and give openly without remorse, drawing strength and conviction from a supernatural force. If I give completely openly, will the world allow me to live free? So much to witness, do, and see. Eternity calls where the darkness is Obsolete, the light of love has no limit, the birds bellow,and The Souls Frolic!!!

When we acknowledge the hoax-wearing mask of our society and begin to unveil our falsities, then and only then can we experience the wonders of the togetherness of humanity.

It's been real. It's been fun. But has it been real fun?

Definitions

1. Living the dream means that someone is living his best life. He is acheiving the goals he wants to acheive. He has all the material, comfort, and/or relationships that he wants to have

2. Grandiose - impressive and imposing to appearance or style, especially pretentiously so
   The court's grandiose facade
   Grandiose plans to reform the world

3. Delusional - Characterized by or holding idiosyncratic beliefs or impressions that are contradicted by reality or rational arguments

4. Creative - Relating to or involving the imagination of original ideas, especially in the production of an artistic work
   Change unleashes people's creative energy

5. Spiritual Warfare-Spiritual warfare is the Christian concept of fighting against the work of preternatural evil forces. It is based on the biblical belief in evil spirits or demons that are said to intervene in human affairs in various ways.

6. Faith - Strong belief in God or in the doctrines of a religion based on spiritual apprehension rather than proof. Delay, trouble, or suffering without getting angry or

upset. Complete trust or confidence in someone or something.

7. Destiny - the events that will necessarily happen to a particular person or place in the future.
8. Loyalty - A strong feeling of support or allegiance.
9. Disease - A change in a living body (as a person or plant) that prevents it from functioning normally: sickness.
10. Respect - A feeling of deep admiration for someone or something elicited by their abilities, qualities, or acheivements.
11. Charismatic - Exercising a compelling charm which inspires devotion in others.
12. Hope - A feeling, an expectation or desire for a certain thing to happen.
13. Grace - Simple eloquence or refinement of movement.
14. Fear - An unpleasant emotion caused by the belief that something or someone is dangerous or likely to cause pain or a threat.

FEAR: FACE EVERYTHING AND RECOVER
FORGET EVERYTHING AND RUN

15. Famous - known about by many people: celebrity.
16. Philanthropist - A person who seeks to promote the welfare of others especially by the generous donations of money to good causes.
17. Empathy - The ability to understand and share the feelings of another.
18. Patience - Capacity to accept or tolerate delay.
19. Humility - the quality or condition of being humble; modest opinion or estimate of one's own importance, rank, etc.
20. Compassion - a feeling of deep sympathy and sorrow for another who is stricken by misfortune, accompanied by a strong desire to alleviate the suffering.
21. Self awareness - conscious knowledge of one's own character, feelings, motives, and desires.
22. Self care - the practice of taking an active role in protecting one's own well-being and happiness, in particular during periods of stress.
23. Respect - esteem for or a sense of the worth or excellence of a person, a personal quality or ability, or something considered as a manifestation of a personal quality or ability.

24. Love - a profoundly tender, passionate affection for another person. A feeling of warm personal attachment or deep affection, as for a parent, child, or friend. Sexual passion or desire.
25. Joy - the emotion of great delight or happiness caused by something exceptionally good or satisfying; keen pleasure; elation. A source or cause of keen pleasure or delight; something or someone greatly valued or appreciated.
26. Peace -the normal, nonwarring condition of a nation, group of nations, or the world. A state of mutual harmony between people or groups, especially in personal relations.
27. Patience - an ability or willingness to suppress restlessness or annoyance when confronted with delay. Quiet, steady perseverance; even-tempered care; diligence.
28. Kindness - having, showing, or proceeding from benevolence. The act of being indulgent, considerate, helpful or humane.
29. Goodness - Moral excellence; virtue. Kindly feeling; kindness; generosity. Excellence of quality. The best part of anything; essence; strength.
30. Faithfulness - Lasting loyalty and trustworthiness in relationships, especially

marriage and friendship. The fact or quality of being true to one's word or commitments, as to what one has pledged to do, professes to believe, etc. The fact or quality of being dedicated and steadfast in performing one's duty, working for a cause, etc. the quality of adhering to fact, a standard, or an original; accuracy.

31. Gentleness - The quality of being kindly; amiable: not severe, rough, or violent; mild: moderate: gradual.
32. Self Control - control or restraint of oneself or one's actions, feelings, etc.

Nuts & Bolts

Turning twenty-one,
I was diagnosed with bipolar type 1
with drastic mood swings, hallucinations, paranoia.
What a crisis. What a mind blowing destroyer.
Existing with mental dis-ease on the planet's
hemisphere and lunar eclipses solar. Would being
chronically mentally ill deny me from achieving my
        goals and reaching far.
The Devil haunted and taunted me once again.
Would this paranoid, lunacy ever end?
For the Love of the Holy Spirit.
When? Oh, when?

Having a flashback of taking an overdose of psych
        pills
placed me on (CO) close observation and suicide
watch. Being plagued with mental illness and
        stigma,
I must protest and march.
All these dual diagnoses are placed by the Devil's
        sweaty palms.
There is no solace amongst the varying people.
The outcome is bleak.
Refuge for the suffering we must seek.
The only saving grace is to capitalize on this disease
and realize its exuberant powers face to face.

All kinds of deadly addictions from food to alcohol
and drugs. They are all frightening disorders.
Why can't we give up the poison
and drink from the holy anointed water?

From January of 2021, for several months
I've been very sick and lost.
I've been like a car that not only needs to replace
the battery, yet also the exhaust.

I broke up with my boyfriend of four and a half
                    years.
We were living together.
This is a perilous storm I might not weather.
I left my boyfriend's apartment, basically homeless,
to visit a shelter and sleep on a cot.
This was a major stressor; too much to handle
without a Klonopin or Ativan, merely a lot.
I was presently not officially working,
trying to publish literary pieces and essays.
My mental and spiritual health were certainly
                    decayed.
Everyone prayed for my well being—would that
ever be what I myself and
the world would be seeing?

As a result of extreme depression, insomnia,
                    exhaustion, and paranoia, I lost control my
                    brand new vehicle,

and drove head on into the Tappan Zee Bridge
or Mario Cuomo Bridge guard rail.
I am lucky I wasn't charged with vehicle
      manslaughter and had to post bail.
It's been so painful, I could sob and wail.
Sometimes I can't fathom if I will ever realize
      all of my dreams and not fail.
Yet my every breath and my life
is the Lord's to do with as he sees fit.
One day I know, definitely speaking,
there will be in heaven a pedestal to sit.
So therefore, no matter how many wind storms
that dare to take me down,
I just won't quit.

Wait, help me, I am having a night terror, a
      flashback
I am under spiritual warfare; a brutal attack.
I was in Westchester Medical Center for two and a
      half weeks
staring at the broken ceilings and walls.
I was peeing in a filthy, dirty bathroom stall,
waiting to take my meds in the unit hall.
They released me to a homeless shelter in the Bronx
with no home in sight.
I was so scared I took a taxi upstate to my mother
      and my brother's.
I couldn't breathe from all my anxiety; I began to
      feel smothered.

I was residing at my mom's tiny apartment
sleeping on a small couch that felt like cement.
I was feeling very confused and lost.
I took a few extra psch pills and my mom called
        911.
The ambulance took me to Mid-Hudson Regional
        Hospital in Poughkeepsie.
I have been admitted to the hospital recently
so many times it was becoming seasonal.
Still depressed, laying in my bed, drooling, wishing
time and time again that I was dead. Disheveled,
meds not level, thinking I was possessed by the
        Devil.
Feeling like a sick freak, a rebel.
Not showering or interacting with the other patients
        on the ward.
Being totally reclusive. Not participating in
        therapeutic groups.
Time going by so slowly.
Extremely tired and bored.
Sleeping most of the days away in the pitch dark.
I hadn't been outside or had fresh air in months.
Dreamed of playing in the park.
Living with mental illness for over thirty years.
I cannot endure or endear.
Placed on more combos of meds than a subway
        hero.
When will all my suffering end?
The doctors claim to know when.

Yet they have no concluding clue.
There's only so much they can do. I tried ECT
(Shock therapy).
Didn't unlock the doors of depression and psychosis
for me.
Unfortunately, it was the wrong key.
Locked up in what seems like solitary
confinement—a prison cell.
How long will the isolative, separate feeling dwell?
God Almighty, hear my prayers.
Save me. I don't feel so well.
Hoist me from this Hell.

The Havoc of Humanity
The Chaos of Calamity
The Rudeness of Vulgarity
The Lucidness of Insanity
The Hospital stays frequently.

Oh, God, hear my prayers.

Don't allow this anguish to settle and dwell.
Oh God, hear my prayers, hoist me from Hell.
My life is so beautiful and spiritually blessed
when I am healthy and well.

God, hear my prayers. Respond
with the heightening angelic church bells.

Bereave Me/Don't Leave Me

Daddy you always made me feel like a little
princess with my glimmering eyes and crown.
The day God took you from my tight, grasping
hands, my joyous aura and smile—
with streams of sobbing tears—
turned to a descending frown.
You echoed and spoke to me so much
        encouragement and love.
Surely, I surmised when the doves of delight
flew in unison, they ascended to the heavens above.
Oh tainted blood, how gruesome it is.
After your open-heart surgery,
they diagnosed you with AIDS.
In my spirit, all the Broadway shows that played
would fade and shut down.
No more star-fested show-biz.
It is what it is.
In the depths of my soul after thirty years
I still ache for your teaching and touch.
Some days the pain I feel is unbearable,
just emotionally and spiritually too much.
God took you home on my seventeenth b-day.
The cake had no icing or fudge.
Will I ever recover from all of this heartache and
        drudge?
My dancing, twirling heart must have given quits.

The cherries I liked to lick are only left with the
pits. Your passing and lasting words were spoken to
me "Princess, I'll buy you whatever you want for
        your B-day when I get out of here."
Just to hear those eloquent words brought a joyful
        tear.
AIDS left you paralyzed and 100 pounds wet.
How could your loved ones not be worried and fret?
I love you now and forever.
The tender, sweet closeness we established will
        never sever.
Rest in peace, Daddy, with God in Heaven's allure
now. Your presence opened my capillaries galore
and your soft element allowed me to realize my
dreams and soar. Keep calling me kiddo, winking at
        me.
Make sure, ultimately, that I am safe and happy
and no longer chained from bondage, free
until we meet again
and I don't know when. Yet til then,
I will cherish the memories that spread like a
rainbow after the storm.
I will always hold dear when we used to bathe in
        the sunlight
where we are eternally protected from harm and
        warm.

Parental Hide-dance

I am jumping and skipping along in my youth.
Eating candy, ice cream, sipping lemonade.
Yet many other youths are experiencing a
        cavalcade,
a raid on their imagination or good sensations.
The cold hard facts: what keeps their dismal lives
        intact?
For me, it is hot air balloons in the sky.
My cherry flavored Italian ice is so good, I could
        cry tears of joy
while I wait to be given from my parents a new toy.
Living my happy childhood.
Thank God that's not a fabricated lie.
I have the inexplicable answers, no need to fathom
        why.
Other youths are being abused, misused, and
        certainly not amused.
Parents don't gently lay them in a sandbox.
But rather cast them in an ironclad intox
with no sight of detox.
These children are lost and irrepressible
with no parental guidance to speak of at all.
If these parents don't change their behavior and
savor being righteous, they will fall prey to
society's call of abandonment and aloneness.
What a raving mess!

How could these children survive on their own?
Who's going to change their diapers?
Who's going to comfort them when they are
sleeping and have a nightmare and moan?
Who's going to clothe and feed them
when the hunger is unspeakable and great?
Please God in Heaven, don't tell me this is a child's
        fatalistic fate.
Will these abusive, neglectful parents get help and
        want to change?
On the charts from one to ten where do they range?
Will they rearrange their life actions and promote
        healthy transactions?
Are the children safe and accounted for?
Can their parents be safe
and not treat them like they're militants in a war?
Can they financially provide for youth's
necessities?
Are the abandonment issues going to seize?
Why, oh why, must this harsh reality make so many
in touch with it cry? These statements evoke and
provoke feelings and emotions
causing mass erosions
All children, first and foremost, deserve the right to
        be loved and to love.
This is God's ultimate message from above.

Spreading like Wildfire:
We Need the Messiah

Crumbling tumbling universe by the second.
Is this the day to reckon.
We might have to beg and beckon
for reconciliation for the nation.
I want to change the face of the world
without plastic surgery.
Yet why has everything plummeted
to the point that we are practically in a state of
        emergency?
Mental illness and addictions are spreading quick.
More and more people becoming sick.
Why do they call them recreational drugs
if there is no recess?
The epidemic is a complex and sad mess.
Now they are using potent fetalyne
to combat harrowing heroin
and using Sombokin to beat opioid addiction.
We need to not cast judgment on
this growing number of people seen as drug fiends.
Methamphetamines amongst the many
seemed to be the current, tragic scene.
This is Satan's mignon. Satan's sin.
Millions affected by mental illness and addiction,
dropping and dying faster than flies
from these atrocities of affliction.

Crumbling, tumbling universe by the second.
Is this the day to reckon with reconciliation of the
nation? Political anarchy at its worst.
Spreading coast to coast
The Presidential campaign between
Joe Biden and Donald Trump was insidiously
insane. People have strong opposing and
contraddicting beliefs. Protests arising all over,
            causing stress and grief.
On January 6th, 2021, violators pouncing on doors
and breaking windows at our nation's Capitol Hill.
Haven't the people of the world been through
enough? Haven't they gotten their fill???
 Where are we Americans safe?
Is it a remote place?
A new destination of freedom and space?
The coronavirus has hit the planet
and so many have been infected.
People will inevitably die.
We ask the Great Creator why.
People for protection wearing masks.
The economy is crashing;
people listing their job's tasks,their livelihood.
The severe ramifications of this virus are
            misunderstood.
Six feet of social distancing, no human touch.
This is all too much.
Shortage of food and cars.
Gas prices at a ridiculous high.

Biden shutdown the pipeline.

People want to know the details of why?

He opened the Mexican borders

to let some illegal immigrants in.

Some smuggling drugs; most looking for new living
quarters.

Dr. Anthony Fauci discovered a vaccine.

Fewer lives lost, positive changes forseen.

The world begins to get back to some semblance of
normalcy

Yet how long will this be?

They try to mandate the vaccine.

For some this is a wise choice.

For others it's obscene.

The Delta and Omicron variants appear.

Once again, the world's living in fear,

watching the saddening statistics on the news.

Is the Government just waiting on cues?

Crumbling tumbling universe by the second.

Is this the day to reckon?

We might have to beg and beckon

for reconciliation of the nation.

Shootings on the rise at schools and on the street.

People falling prey to being victims of violent
defeat.

Putin's behavior and actions are maniacal, more like
Hitler.

He never deserves the respect

or to be addressed as Sir.

Ukraine is under severe attack.

There's no going back.

That's a cold brutal fact.

Too many innocent children and people are dying.

So many people in the world left crying.

What's going on in Ukraine is insane.

How will they be able to sustain and maintain
their freedom and rights?

Do any of you bystanders have any insight?

War always at the core erupts from power and
        greed.

Yet with world peace, the evil sinners who lead will
not succeed.

Crumbling, tumbling universe of ours.

Our Father who art in heaven. Hallowed be thy
        name.

Our world is under attack by the enemy
that those spiritual believers can surely see.

We must ban together in warfare to break free.

Prevent lives being lost at any cost.

Crumbling, tumbling universe of ours.

The Surreal Deal/
Call from Grace Part Two

I was placed in the gates of Hell.
I wasn't surviving so well.
If I made it out alive, I would have much to tell.
It was a true wrath of insanity.
I wouldn't partake in this ambush of humanity.
Wouldn't be cruel or hold dearly to vanity.
Where I was temporarily residing had a fearful and
        unsafe enmeshment of a brutal calamity.
Reality-based truth of the lowest functioning and
sickest people with mental dis-ease.
This pathetic parallel was more than just a tease
and its repercussions would linger on, it wouldn't
cease. These poor souls have no ambitions, hopes or
goals. Every day was the same. It was boring and
        tame.
It needed to be reframed.
Begging and pleading for food and money.
It was beyond harrowing. It certainly wasn't funny,
smoking cigarettes, digging through the garbage
        pails and ashtrays for more, abusing weed,
drinking alcohol which would impede.
Their addictions, they couldn't concede.
Garbage thrown all over the ground.
They thought the sanitation department was going
to come around and pick up what they found.

I tried to change them and lead.
All they wanted was to have food to feed
their hungry bodies and minds.
They were in vegatative states,
not much for me to converse about or find.
I swore I'd be kind.
I had never witnessed anything like this nor would I
     want to again.
Mental illness and addictions had become an
epidemic, When would its life-altering devastations
     end?
Yet mental disorder or not, I wouldn't live this fate.
I wouldn't give up on love yell disgusting
     profanities
or beat other humans in hate
I was living within the entrappings of the police's
     stomping grounds.
There was no peace, only loud pathetic sounds.
The residents didn't shower. The men wouldn't
shave. Most of them didn't want to be saved
or act appropriately and behave.
They knew nothing of God,
clueless of the meaning behind the staff and the rod.
Most of the residents preached a good game,
yet their lives would lay dormant.
Their lives would remain the same.
They shit and peed on the floors,
also on the bathroom doors.
I was there for five weeks and couldn't take it any

more.
Most of the men were ex-convicts,
drug dealers and users.
Most of them were society's abusers.
 I couldn't find refuge or peace of mind to do my
        writings;
to share and give to Mother Earth.
I couldn't continue my evolution
and have continual rebirth or spiritual growth.
I wanted out of this hellhole.
That was my sole goal.
It was like a tiny fish bowl.
It was beginning to affect me negatively
and take a mental and spiritual toll.
I had already suffered
to the point, God forbid, of no return.
I had to move forth.
There was more to teach and more to learn.
I had to master from the Creator how to discern.
I had to discern how to create my own destiny.
How to unlock doors even with no key.
I would be one in sync
with the Father, The Holy Ghost, and the Son.
When all was said and done,
I work primarily for the Kingdom.
No need to be scared and run.

The Lord's arms are wide open to grab me tight.
He will deliver repentance to my insight.

During times of darkness, He shines His bright
light. Society is locked away in a system of decay.
What more do I have to expand on and say?
We have to rid ourselves of our greed and
selfishness and ban together today.
We have to work hard at change
and reconstruction with no abruption
and steadfastly pray. I see no other way.
We can't stand idle or at bay. Do you want to lay?
Lay down and give in to insurmountable sin?
It always comes down to free will.
Yet, without a revelation or revolution
in no time at all, will we exist still?
The choice is yours. Develop your core.
Take God's path, not the Devil's detour.
Now you understand what all the righteous
            believers are fighting for.

Where I was residing, I needed to leave this
            outrage,
this unbearable cage.
I needed to move forth, to continue my quest.
I knew in my insatiable soul that this would be best.
I took the horse by the reins.
No longer was I going to be judged as delusional,
insane. My mother once said to me that if I didn't
promise to try and get better, I'd end up in a State
Hospital for the rest of my life with murderers and
            the criminally insane.

This sentence wasn't fair, considering all I ever
dreamed about from a young age was to be ordained
and to establish fame within my calling.
So why was I continually placating,
playing the victim role and stalling?
My high school English teacher said to me,
"All those days, all those hours,
all that talent cast aside. You must get going."
It was time for me to stop being so afraid of failure
on my journey, my riveting ride.
To stop slowing down my destiny,
slowing down my opportunity.
To soar like a bald eagle and be rightfully free.
Instead, I was feeling like Jesus Christ,
crucified and bloodstained
Now was the time to show the world
that I was perfectly sane;
running gloriously like a horse with its mane.
Driving quickly yet cautiously in the right lane.
I believe God and my deceased loved ones from
Heaven led me to a place I could leaven.

I met Ms. MM and I instantaneously knew
she would become my angel by my side.
She was such a human essence, I almost cried—
cried tears of happiness.
With me living on her estimated 30 million dollar
           mansion estate grounds, I surely wouldn't
           digress.

On the contrary, I would progress.
She gave me an opportunity to relive my fairytale
        childhood and also begin anew.
I wanted this reality through and through.
I'd do whatever I had to do
to permeate within this magical state of mind.
I'd discover all of life's purposeful dreams.
I sensed Ms. MM was truly kind.
When we met, we had a lot in common.
Her adorable ten year old daughter rode horses
and so did I at that age.
Maybe it was time to turn the page
backward and remember the childhood fairytale.
I once had lived with an expensive toy box and
        many Barbie dolls.
I could not allow myself to get so depressed and sad
for my many losses and remorses
suffering and pain; the intensity
of all I battled and sustained.
Ms. MM and I would share a kinship.
Yet I'd be on my best behavior
and watch my words that came out of my lip.
I'd keep proper boundaries
and not reveal my whole existence at once.
It could take months.
Sometimes the less you know about a person
the better for all.
It was time to stand up straight, not slouch and fall.

Ms. MM was a well-known New York socialite
and had acheived greatness with her companies,
philanthropie, and artwork.
Her quintessential talent was so mind boggling, it
was a given that, close by, God did lurk.

The land Lord of all creation
was part of this divine intervention.
I'd finally completely excellerate,
reach my fate,
and be forgiven for all my sins
complete and utter redemption.

I would wake up on the estate grounds to a piece of
          heaven; a complete sanctuary.
The birds were bellowing songs of praise to the
Creator, I felt like I was on my way to the
penthouse suite in the Euphoric Elevator.
I could hear the wind chimes in harmony.
I could see the sunrise and it was like seeing the
          Son rise.
I knew, finally, I had given myself permission
to be all that I could be.
Ms. MM was strict with her privacy and
          boundaries.
It was a good lesson for me
because maintaining proper boundaries
was a matter I've been working on for years.

I had to believe I could accomplish my dreams
independently without so many fears.
When she showed me the apartment,
she said, "this is your world
and my world is mine."
I surmised what she was actually saying
was the two wouldn't align.
Yet our meeting was certainly a greater sign.
She had made her mark on society sooner than I.
Had children and husbands. I didn't,
and couldn't understand why?
Perhaps one day, our worlds would collide
and, once again, this angel would be by my side.
In the interim, I'd admire and respect her from afar

I know in my heart that each human being,
with God's help, can shine like a star.
They are bewildered and cry out to God above.
The saints are marching in sync.
Can you imagine that glorious vision?
What do you think?

Ms. MM's mansion was flooded
with gorgeous and expensive antiques.
My father was an antique dealer and, as a young
        girl,
I would accompany him on house calls and to work.
I truly believe my new living quarters were
predestined. Do you think I am a freak?

I am finally calm like a holy psalm.
I finally can breathe and not feel suffocated,
the Holy Spirit within me.
This is my life long decree.
This is what I studied and experienced hard.
This is my degree.
I will wave my ethereal fairy princess wand
 and attempt to touch the minds and hearts of each
          lost soul.
This will be my ultimate role.
I will play it with grace. I will play it with class.
And I will continue to be a "Royal Pain in the
          Ass!!!"

Belle of the Ball

Princess Tessa Rose galivants into the sunlit hall.
The Autumn leaves are changing to brilliantly
        defining colors.
It is the beginning of Fall.
A new season. A hopeful, enchanting reason
that she will come upon her prince.
It's been so long since she felt appreciated and
adored. The allure. What adventure is in store?
Princess Tessa Rose is dressed in her finest Vera
        Wang gown.
Wearing, in addition, a shimmering smile; kissing
goodbye to yesteryear's fruitless frown.
Princess Tessa Rose was determined to meet her
prince and they would become renowned.
She experienced many frogs, turds from her past.
 She was ready for a new beginning.
The disappointment wouldn't last.
She prayed by the waterfall
as the angels cascaded down from the altar above.
They bathed her in the amazing possibility of
        eternal love.
Princess Tessa Rose remembers, as a little girl
dreaming under the moonlit stars, that one day
Prince Charming would be waiting for her.
She would be decked out in fine jewelry and fur.
They'd waltz to the magic of the music,

connecting, swaying step by step
with anticipated enthusiasm and pep;
ultimately having a ball.
As a little girl, she would wait for the Godly call.
Her soulmate was a call of fate.
Princess Tessa Rose wanted him to be punctual, not
late. The prince would be worth the long, drawn out
process. The wailing wait.
Her mother and father showed her what it meant
to be a royal couple displaying majestic bliss.
Devoted and truly dedicated to one another.
The Princess was enamored by her entire family,
immediate and distant. Especially her father, mother
and brother.
Along Princess Tessa Rose's chariot ride,
due to life choices and complications,
she didn't bear children or find marriage.
What a painful surprise.
She succumbed to men that didn't know the first
requirement of respecting her
or taking the hand of a "Classy Dame."
Now and then a nice guy came.
These regal, kind men along the way were special.
Yet she knew in her heart that the feelings she
developed toward them wouldn't stay.
When Princess Tessa Rose finally met the one,
they would gaze into each other's lucid eyes.
There will be only lasting "hello's"
He would kiss her on her lip.

They would toast with champagne and slowly,
       succently sip.
The Prince would caress her, undress her,
lay her bare on the bed.
Princess Rose's spirit would be solely fed
and her Prince would put a diamond ring on her
finger, and they would say, "I do"
to all of their dreams and wed.

Weigh In/Way Out

If I choose to weigh in, is there a way out?
Am I just a fixated number on the scale?
If I don't fit into (no pun intended)
society's normal size, does that mean I fall?
Since I was ten years old, I have been compulsively
binging, regurgitating, and at times vegetating and
isolating which leads to lacking in self-esteem.
The cycle of insanity can make me scream.
Definition of insanity (extreme foolishness or
        irrationality)
Was being chubby, overweight, fat, obese
looked upon as being a cultural, cynical, cult?
Am I not good enough or whole?
Should I shut down my savoring soul?
I feel ugly and unacceptable.
Yet I am a receptacle for growth and change.
It's my negative thinking and unhealthy lifestyle
I am determined to rearrange.
Regardless of my size, color of my eyes, hair color
        and style,
I am a child of the most high which makes me
        wondrously worthwhile.
I am beautiful inside and out.
Yet, I have had in the past of many opposing bouts
of self-deprecation despair, depression, and
        regression.

It is my time to fly, spread my wings,
harmoniously sing.
I now choose to live healthy, be wealthy.
Physically, emotionally, spiritually and flee
from the bondage of distorted body image, I am
         free.
I am so much more than a number on a scale or an
outer shell to be harshly judged.
I righteously deserve to be loved and to love.
Once upon a rhyme and time, the food addiction
added to the restriction of my dreams.
However, now my screams of insanity have become
         calm and quiet.
I will no longer fall victim to crazy diets.
Being mind, body, spirit sound,
it's become a way of survival;
a reopening revival.
An endurance of courage and resilience.
Taking hold of God's healing power and brilliance.
Ah men!
(so be it)
See it!

Pick the Winning Motto Number

Spin the wheel!
This will be a life altering experience
That your whole being will feel.
It's time to count the poker chips and deal.
Jesus was a prophet who performed miracle after
miracle and was a well known leading rabbi who
held many lectures and discussions, bringing the
people
tears of joy, yet also to cry. Jesus was undoubtedly
the Son of God, the Messiah.
That is why He would eventually
recreate the nations and live in Heaven, up high.
When He was brutally crucified by the Pharisees,
which brought him to the Romans, He was a mere
thirty three years of age. It was at the same time that
the Devil would become bitter and enraged and
chained to a fire bearing pit of a cage.
The Israelites were exiled from Egypt to the barren
desert for forty years,
their persecutors sincere.
The Israelites quivered with fear.
144,000 people divided by the twelve tribes of
Israel.
If only all of the observers and viewers could read
the Bible
and fully digest this cryptic and fascinating

tale.

666 for the foolish, naive, manipulative, deceitful,
and narcisistic might be the winning Motto number.

Hopefully Satan will stay in a paralyzing dark
slumber.

It is the mark of the Beast and at the start of a new
world.

666 will no longer make us all sick sick sick.

Satan won't be cordially invited to the Lord's and
lamb's holy feast.

He will be tortured in a pit of flames.

There will be a seal to contain.

No way for the Devil to escape the burning and
boils. Jesus will be the King of New Creation part
of the Euphoric Royals.

No more putting 666 on humans' right hands and
foreheads.

No more tears, crying, pain, or suffering.

The old ways have passed away and are dead.

Lastly, the happpenings of the horrific bombing of
N.Y. City's Twin Towers

is strangely enough going on the 20th anniversary
of its occurrence.

It makes no Godly sense.

That fatal reality was more condensed.

The amount of killings was beyond intense.

Now count to ten.

1, 2, 3, 4, 5, 6, 7, 8, 9. 10.

Oh, all of this preposterous evil.

When will we heal and when will it end
for all innocent women and men?

Yummy Tummy/The Last Supper

Emmanuel is the Alpha and the Omega.
The begginning and the end
On Judgment Day, he will save us from our sins.
He will act as the trial lawyer and defend
the perpetrators and see who is innocent and wins.
I will pick up a good non-fiction book,
perhaps the Book of Life.
It will store accurate and predestined names:
Daughters, Sons, Fathers, Mothers,
perhaps Groom and Wife.
His Angels will play the instruments so heavenly
for all the earth to witness, listen too, and see.
Jesus is to appear in the translucent, white clouds.
He will beckon to His servants and worshippers out
loud. The Lord will have bronze feet.
He will climb up on his emperor's throne.
There will be an assigned seat.
He will wear a linen and silk robe and gold crown
All of creation with think this vision
is a magical feat performed by the psuedomagican
with a wand witnessed by the town parliament.
The Lord will create new, glorious existence of
faith, grace, and fate
for all those people who are saved.
Each individual at the Holy Feast
will have so much to boast about and rave.

Satan will be put in his place by the lake with fire.
He will be stripped of his evil desires.
After all he is a bastard, a narcissistic liar.
He will also be stripped of his cruelty,
left naked with only leaves— no attire.
He will be tortured and condemned to Hell for
1,000 years.
All of us humans will have no more darkness to
fear.
Jesus will mend and rectify all evil
and join all His people in heaven
and be a Godly light.
I am exhilarated to have this insight and foresight.
Spread the word about Revelation of Jesus and the
Holy Gate in New Jerusalem.
If you suffered for the sake of Jesus,
you will be rewarded.
All of these occurrences were predestined and
prerecorded.
All we are really here on earth for is to evolve, heal,
and comfort people by example;
to direct them towards the ok corral of Heaven.
If you don't evolve you dissolve.
Thank the Lord we are given time to resolve.

Playtime with Riddles and Rhymes

Swinging tall and high
above the bright blue sky.
Only happy thoughts.
No time for temper tandrums and to cry.
The merry go round
goes around at rapid speeds and
is fast. The memories I am
gathering in the willow tree festooned
park today will surely stay ingrained
in my heart and last.
Eating Rocky Road, Pink Bubble gum, and Oreo
      Cookie ice cream.
My playmates and I
are quite the infantile team.
It's time to run to the balance beam.
Why does the innocence and fun of childhood have
      to end?
It's so glorious to make new friends!
Why can't I race around and soar forever more?
As time travels on, I must be responsible
and live from my adult core.
Back to running around the park and drinking
      lemonade.
Please God, don't take away this amazing reality
      and let it fade.
The ice cream truck has stopped at a red light,

tempted to give my inner child a bite
even if I have to fight.
I'll have my chocolate M&M's.
I'll take a lasting bite.
My playmate in the sandbox, Jesus Christ,
supplies all of the footprints and light.

White Clouds and Unicorns

By Mary Mercurio
And Sarai London Tailor

White clouds & unicorns as I drift off to sleep.
Dancing clowns and candy corn are waiting there
       for me.

Lollipops and puppy dogs. I reach for my brass
       ring.
Merry go rounds and pools of blue. I splash and
       laugh and sing.

White clouds and unicorns puff my pillow up for
       me.
A cotton candy under my shirt only for me to see.

Jesus walks in front, beside, behind as I drift off to
white clouds and unicorns that guard my destiny.

My Darling Sweetness

"Life is a flower of which love is the honey"

I will never forget or stop cherishing the way you
        caressed me
when we snuggled and with kindness, loyalty, and
        caring, you addressed me.
Your smile is contagious.
You valued me, treated me like a lady
and made me feel outrageous.
You were my first long-lasting, balanced, stable
        relationship
in all of my adult life and,
even after being together for years,
I relished in our companionship
and didn't find it necessary to become your wife.
Some days were more romantic, rambunctious, and
rewarding than others with less strife.
You constantly surprised me with flowers and gifts
        galore.
You respected me sexually
and didn't expect me to act like a sex worker nor
        whore.
You have captivated the depths of my soul and core.
You were my fellah and I was your dame.
I enjoyed the affection
when you had an erection

and those days when you ejaculated and came.
Foreplay, five play, was a strategic game.
Your humor had me in hysterics and stitches.
Laughing so hard felt better than acquiring all the
world's riches.
Your knowledge about trivia, music, and sports
were impressive.
Your constant babbling about who you knew on
Facebook
was annoying and excessive.
I will always be thankful to your special family.
They accepted me in all my entirety and let me be.
They were understanding of all my mental health
issues and episodes.
They stayed positive and didn't allow my mind to
erode. Although we've decided to only be friends,
I love you very, very much and that will never end.
As you continue to travel on your life path,
may you hold dear even with past mistakes;
how far you have come
and know in your spirit how you made me feel
connected as if we were one.
"Remember life is a flower in which love is the
honey."
I pray hard that our ongoing days will bring
fortitude and be sunny!

Rainbow

Sit Down Comedian

My inner child is provoked and evoked, going wild.
My mood and actions are hypomanic. More or less
mild. A surge in creativity, a splurge in comedy
for all the world to chuckle and see.
To laugh in the belly until it hurts.
Do I require a spiritual and mental alert?
Am I getting, God forbid, dangerously manic again?
When, oh when, will this end?
Will anyone tell me the truth?
Am I being promiscuous; flirting with everyone
and fantasizing about sleeping around town? Am I
extremely hyper and happy with no sight of a
     frown?
Am I spending money aimlessly?
Do I still comprehend that some things are free?
Am I talking rapidly and quick?
Please God in Heaven, keep me from again getting
     sick.

I'll tell you a joke
if you pour me a diet Coke,
share a smoke.
I may even toke
now that pot is legal,
may even be regal

If you don't care for the jokes, tell me I need new
material and say it out loud
in front of the crowd.
Don't disregard my tip jar,
After all, I AM A CZAR
that will conquer evil and go far.
That may or may not sound bizarre.
Yet, let's get on with the show before it gets too late
and you'll have to go.

1. How do you know the man liked fruit? He
   had an Apple computer.
2. She liked to dabble in playing scrabble so
   her life didn't become a bored game.
3. If I was a polar bear, how would I say bye?
   Bipolar.
4. Can a maintenance man maintain his
   relationship? If he screws.
5. Does a bear need oxygen? If he is barely
   breathing.
6. I have my menstrual cycle, does that mean I
   will have PMS (Permissible Manslaughter)?
7. What did the seven foot man do when the
   waitress took his order? He put in a tall
   order.
8. The math teacher was horny and had four
   play. She added one partner and had five
   play.
9. What temperature do you put your stove on
   when you are cooking a pot pie? High.

10. What did the woman do when she needed a new tire for her car? She went clothes shopping and got a new attire

11. What did the dog tell the treatment he likes to do? (Bark)

12. The psychiatrist asked me if I hear voices. I said I hear my mom constantly screaming at me

13. What is a Messianic Jew? A mess of a Jew.

14. How did she know she was nuts? She kept eating cashews, almonds, and pecans.

15. How was the priest when he played golf? He got a Holy in one.

16. What did the blind man do? He went to swim in the sea.

17. How do you know Godiva chocolate is the best? It comes from God.

18. How did the female cop keep her boobs from sagging? She was in a hold up.

19. What happened when the man fell? He said he was falling for me.

20. What happened to the happy jeweler? He shined like a diamond.

21. Although Mary was a virgin. Jesus is coming.

22. Was the strawberry tasty? It was berry good.

23. How did she know she liked to sleep with artists? She had drawers.

24. I took my mom out to lunch. I used my corporate credit card to pay. Now, I could finally write her off.
25. I went to see the chiropractor. He told me he was all skin and bones.
26. I keep telling my boyfriend how important he is. Yet in reality, he was impotent. Now he's my ex.
27. My brother was an accountant. He told me our relationship was getting taxing.
28. I went to see my dentist. He had more plaques on the wall than I had in my mouth.
29. I met a guy that does construction. He asked me what type of work I wanted done. I said I would start with the boobs and the face.
30. My dentures started falling out. So my mom told me to use Poly Grip. I told her, "if this was your reality, you would have to get a grip."
31. What size Yeshua does Jesus wear???
32. Jesus was having vision problems. So he went to an optometrist. The optometrist said, "Jesus we are going to have to do a full examination." The doctor examined Jesus and said, "Jesus, I think I know what the problem is. I believe you are Cross eyed.
33. I was given a SAG Award. I unfortunately realized it wasn't because I was talented, it

was because I was over fifty and gravity had taken hold of parts of my body.

34. I was admitted to a psychiatric unit in the hospital. They told me I was a risk of elopement. I blàtantly answered, "you must be kidding me. Look around, there's certainly no eligible bachelors here!!!"

35. As for those Jewish people and equestrians, I accompanied my mother to the horse stable. I suggested she cantor with the Rabbi.

36. I was worried that if I quoted the Bible I would get sued for copyright infringement. But what could possibly happen? A prophet suing me for profit?

37. Either way I win. If I am called back to Heaven, I have many people waiting for me. If I am destined to stay on Earth I have many people waiting on me.

Hope you enjoyed the show! Blessings to you and your loved ones. I pray you had fun. Spread the word. Soon enough I am taking my act on the road.

Warm Regards,
Ms. Lori Eve Tatarsky AKA
Ms. Sarai London Tailor

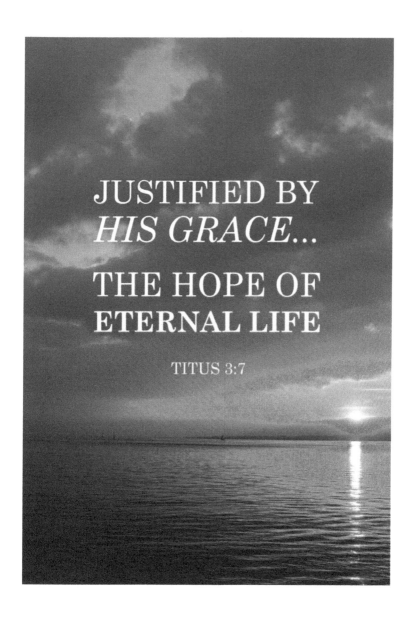

JUSTIFIED BY
HIS GRACE...

THE HOPE OF
ETERNAL LIFE

TITUS 3:7

The End, or Perhaps the Beginning

Revelation 21:4

And God shall wipe away all tears from their eyes and there shall be no more death, neither sorrow nor crying. Neither shall there be any more pain, for the former things are passed away.

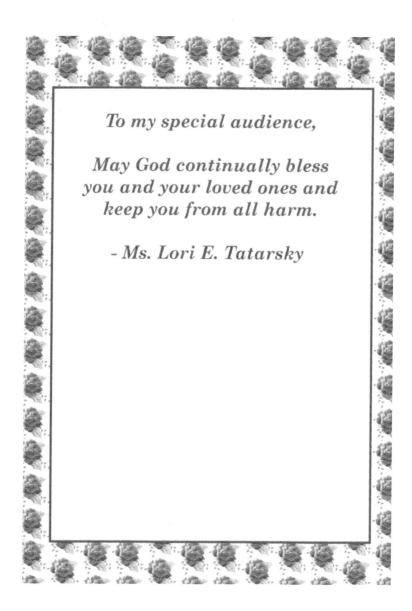

To my special audience,

May God continually bless you and your loved ones and keep you from all harm.

- Ms. Lori E. Tatarsky

About the Author

I was born two and half months premature; glitz and
glamor galore. So many people to learn from and adore.
Never settling for less, always wanting more. Ready,
determined to set this world on fire.
One of my quests was to inspire, to remove society's
hoax-wearing mask. To be genuine, not a liar.
To ultimately keep ascertaining my goals and passions.
To spiritually reach new gains higher and higher. I was
placed not in a manger, but an incubator. And my place
in this world was to be a lover of life, not a hater, due
solely because of choice in the creator.
I truly believe my life was predestined from my first
Passover Seder. The first of my many dreams was
realized 20 years later. Dreams in the making!
Detours, cracked sidewalks, closed doors, pitfalls,
staring at bleak hospital walls, rises and falls, devils
deceiving, devastation, God's many calls.

I am victorious and blessed through it all.
Writing, singing since I was a little girl.
Telling jokes, rebelling, sometimes dwelling in temper
tantrums. Selling, wheeling, dealing, finagling, spieling,
quelling, creating fellowship, and storytelling. Always
mesmerized by the beauty of words. None were too long
or complicated to be heard. Adored play-on-words and
puns—so much fun. Rhymes riddles gave me belly
laugh giggles.
Played dress-up and would act, wanted to provoke and
evoke emotions in others to see them react. Loved to
perform and entertain. To put on impromptu Broadway
shows. It would have been nice if it was money the
recipients chose to throw.
My brother Gil-Gil would play the piano and I would
sing. We imagined we were Donnie and Marie—for all
of our relatives and friends to see.
I was a rebel with a cause of human rights, I craved
universal insight and light.
No matter how long it took, I would fight the good fight.
[From the very first day on this earthly plane, I had
grand-slam ideas and I knew I could live them if I held
on to God's tight grip and overcame my barriers of my
fears. And I could exclaim]
From the very first day on this earthly plane, I had a
flight of ideas, bursting to exclaim. There are myriad
fears, stuffing, stopping, starving, staving
Our true potential through the years.
To breathe free, with God's hand, just be.
"BE NOT AFRAID!"

11/12/22

To my Dear Nancy, who greets me so pleasantly in the morning: "How are you doing?" So far so good! You have such a beautiful positive Aura that envelops. All, you are a kind and altruistic soul, that I am proud to know and have as a friend. Keep enjoying God's wonder with your hikes and Nature.

Thank you for being one of my first readers to support my life mission of transformation.

Much ♥

Ms. Lori Eve Tatarsky
AKA
Ms. Sarai London Tai

Made in the USA
Coppell, TX
19 July 2022